The Pearls of Business

The Pearls of Business

GUIDING PRINCIPLES TO
HELP ENTREPRENEURS
SUCCESSFULLY LAUNCH
AND GROW A GOVERNMENT
CONTRACTING BUSINESS

Jay Newkirk

Foreword by Larry Womack

JAY NEWKIRK
BUSINESS CONSULTING
Dream. Plan. Succeed.

Huntsville, Alabama

The Pearls of Business: Guiding Principles to Help Entrepreneurs Successfully Launch and Grow a Government Contracting Business

ISBN-13: 978-1-7362647-0-6

I dedicate this book to my wife and lifetime partner, Linda.

Table of Contents

Part One: Founding Principles

Part Two: Launch Point

Part Three: Operating Principles and Business Processes

Part Four: Stabilize and Anchor

Part Five: Accelerating Growth and Company Value

Foreword

Jay Newkirk's *The Pearls of Business* is an in-depth, comprehensive, systematic approach to business success that recognizes the importance of human capital. Though drawn primarily from Jay's experiences in government contracting, *Pearls* is a valuable guide for anyone starting or desiring to grow a business or enterprise.

In *Pearls,* Jay skillfully identifies each step required for business success and personal accomplishment. It begins with how to create an attainable dream and ultimately leads to achieving your unique goal and desired financial reward. He writes, "Launching a business and successfully growing it to your desired value proposition is balancing art, people skills, and making optimized, timely, and creative decisions while maintaining a focus on achieving your dream. This is no small feat, but it is absolutely attainable with the right attitude and accessible guidance."

Part One presents the steps for creating the foundations for success and explores the issues faced during the initial launch period. Part Two demonstrates how to define and refine that most important personal dream. Not business goals or objectives, but your personal dream. It also takes a look at the issues faced during a company's launch. Part Three details the structure of a written success plan, including developing long-term goals, vision and mission statements, and a business plan, while covering various operating principles and business processes that are important to have in place. Part Four adroitly expands on the operating principles and business processes necessary to stabilize and anchor your company and drive it deep before you go wide. Part Five demonstrates how to accelerate growth and assess that growth from the perspective of your original business idea and the business plan projections.

By combining his personal experiences and proven practices with innovative concepts and ageless wisdom, *The Pearls of Business* is a roadmap to success. The detailed accounts of the opportunities, barriers, pitfalls, and successes Jay and his team faced are covered with engaging prose, making *Pearls* an accessible, informative read. However, I recommend reading *Pearls* with a highlighter to keep track of the nuances and pithy wisdom found on every page. Most business advice books focus solely on process; *Pearls* weaves the human element throughout. Jay correctly points out that "Whatever product or service your business offers, its ultimate success will come from its people's successful collaboration. How you lead is as important as what you do."

In *The Pearls of Business,* the whetstone for preparing for personal and business success, Jay Newkirk presents *all* the elements required for significant accomplishment. And he does so in an engaging, thoughtful, and compelling manner. *The Pearls of Business* is a must-read for budding entrepreneurs and inspired business leaders.

Larry Womack

Introduction

Launching a business and successfully growing it to your desired value proposition is a balance of art; people skills; and making optimized, timely, and creative decisions while maintaining a focus on achieving your dream. This is no small feat, but it is absolutely attainable with the right attitude and accessible guidance.

Growing up in a small family business, watching my parents succeed and sometimes struggle over time led me to entrepreneurship. In fact, even as a teenager I had a dream to help grow the family business into a significant one with me at the helm. But, parents in the late fifties and early sixties were encouraging their kids to go to college, get a degree, and "get a good job." So, that's what I did.

However, the passion for having my own business never left me. For many years I was living, as Henry David Thoreau put it, "a life of quiet desperation." Following my work on the "Man to the Moon" Apollo Program, I was ready for a change. While continuing my daytime Information Technology (IT) career, some colleagues and I launched a multi-level direct marketing business and we grew it to a significant enough level that to continue it would have required us to work it full time.

Much to our surprise, the multi-level business came under attack. The claims were that it was an illegal pyramid scheme and we lost 30 percent of our business overnight. The business was proven legitimate, but the damage had been done. Soon after that, my partner, Bobby Bradley, and I decided to launch a professional services company based on our educational backgrounds and using what we had learned in our multi-level business experience. Computer Systems Technology, Inc. (CST) was born.

When we launched CST, we had the right attitudes and understood many of the principles I offer in *The Pearls of Business,* but we had to search for guidance. Traditional business books and consultants focused on processes and "how to." We already knew the "how-to" when it came to starting our business. What we needed was to learn the "how-to" when it came to excelling with a winning attitude and ensuring that we kept our eyes on our dream.

During the multi-level direct marketing business period we discovered books by Napoleon Hill, Zig Ziglar, Denis Waitley, Dr. Robert Schuller, Dr. Wayne Dyer, Neil Eskelin, Larry Womack, and Dale Carnegie, among others. Reading their books and working nights and weekends for eight years, helping people learn to dream and teaching them to lead through motivation, grounded us in the essence of winning and success in the free enterprise system. The "pearls of business" were taking shape, though I didn't know it yet. So, after launching CST we set a goal to build it to $100 million annual revenue and 1,000 employees in ten years and then sell it—we actually accomplished that in fourteen.

The Pearls of Business Series

Through experience, diligence, and the willingness and ability to learn, we discovered at CST how to overlay timeless guiding principles with the operational aspects of running a business. We learned how to "hold hands and run" with the people on our teams; we discovered the benefits of surrounding ourselves with people who were better than we were in the areas we needed strengthening, and so forth. Through applying these one-liners in this unique way, we successfully grew our business and saw it through to a very profitable liquidity event. So these principles became

The Pearls of Business as a tool to show others how they, too, can apply these pearls and win.

After several years of informal counseling and consulting with individuals who knew or had heard about my role in helping to successfully grow CST, I realized that there was enough interest in our accomplishment that writing about what we did made sense as I continued to want to help entrepreneurs and business leaders grow and succeed with their own companies.

The original idea relative to the title and the pearls came from understanding that there were some basic truisms and strategies we employed during our CST days that helped capture the essence of our "stepwise" success. The pearls of wisdom I uncovered while reading various books by thought leaders became *The Pearls of Business*. I took these pearls one step further and overlaid them onto business practices. As I've coached and advised others, these pearls, which include quotes from well-known thought leaders, substantiate my guidance.

As I finalized the book's outline and content, I revisited how CST progressed from launch to the liquidity event. As the writing and editing commenced, I decided to include some guidance on how to actually apply the subtle motivational meaning captured in the pearls during the various steps of a business's growth from launch to a liquidity event. As a result, each part of the original book structure has become a standalone book, so *The Pearls of Business* has become a series of books.

The intent of *The Pearls of Business* series is to share with you basic operational principles that, if applied to running and growing your own business and your life, for that matter, will lead to extraordinary success.

My hope is that *The Pearls of Business* series will serve as the missing link between the existing "how-to" books out there and those business leaders who are hungry to learn how to do business differently, better, and with a more positive attitude than their competitors. Internalizing and practicing these timeless guiding principles can only lead to business success and achieving your dream. And isn't that what it's all about?

FOUNDING PRINCIPLES

P art One provides an overview of basic leadership principles that must be practiced in order to have true business success. This important set of success principles must overlay everything you do and what you say and how you say it during all the engagements you have throughout the life of your business. The principles I am referring to and which I will expand on in this section include: The Human Element, The Importance of Having a Dream, Outcome Management, and Getting Inside People's Heads. Part One closes with a discussion of applying what I've coined the SMART Approach to Business Success.

It is important that you understand something about me and why writing this book is so important. I have been thinking about doing this for a long time and I've wanted to somehow share with business owners and entrepreneurs that there are some basic success principles that I have applied in my business life that are absolutely critical to business and personal success. I have needed to share the importance of applying them to every business action and decision. Over time I have shared them with folks in casual conversations and even in counseling sessions, but I've felt that I have fallen short reaching a significant number of the young and excited new business owners and leaders out there that need this knowledge. Reading this book will introduce you to these principles and, if you grasp them, internalize them, practice them, and have success as a result, you will have fulfilled my dream.

As you read, keep in mind that these founding principles are *always* applicable, at every stage of business, no matter what is going on in the world. The trick is learning them, applying them, and figuring out how to adapt them on an ongoing basis even as environments shift and changes take place like during the COVID-19 pandemic we experienced worldwide early in 2020.

That fact leads to an example of the importance of applying these critical principles regardless of environmental changes. How we conduct business now has been impacted greatly by the fact that our nation and the world have undergone a historic event that essentially shut down the world's economy. The event created the need to rethink how we conduct business in an environment where personal contact must be minimized in order to prevent the spread of a deadly virus.

The business principles, the pearls, that are discussed here in Part One, and in the book as a whole, will require careful assessment relative to how they are applied in the future as a result of the increased focus on conducting business virtually.

I also want you to know that I am in this situation with you. I am currently engaged in helping my son grow an information technology government professional services company, Government Energy Solutions, Inc. I'm leading the company's corporate strategy and the development of marketing material and the website while also supporting new business development. As a result, I'm having to learn how best to apply these principles myself with this generation of leaders and how to deal with adapting ways to motivate new workforces in this evolving work environment.

The bottom line is that we all are having to learn that there will be some impacts on applying these basic success principles during our interpersonal engagements now, relative to the proximity distancing we must practice with people, but I know that these principles must be—and still can be—applied. Since a lot of engagements will be via social media and the use of virtual meeting platforms, we will need to discover and find innovative approaches to applying the human element strategy, how to hold on to your dream and promote dream building, and how to apply outcome management techniques continually. There will be some challenges relative to observing body language and perhaps facial expression but applying these success principles I'm going to discuss in this part remains vital to our success. Therefore, application of them will require some practice and closer attention to multimedia and virtual screen images during interchanges, but it can be accomplished with dedication and practice. Now, with that said, enjoy Part One of *The Pearls of Business*.

The Importance of
Having a Dream

I always ask people what their dream is. Why is this important? It's simple: Launching and growing a business is an art and requires a balance between tactical and strategic thinking.

Before continuing I want to make sure you understand what I mean by having a dream. First, it's important not to confuse having a dream with having a goal or company objective. Company goals and objectives are extremely important, but what I am referring to is overlaying all of that with why you started a business in the first place. The dream is personal, it's the reason you stepped away from a job and launched a business. Here's how I want you to think about your dream: if you have had total success with your business and you have a successful liquidity event and become financially free, your dream is what you are going to do with these financial resources and your life. If you structure your personal dream correctly as well as your company's ultimate goals and objectives, the resulting successful liquidity event will result in you achieving your dream.

If you don't have a dream in place, you can't work to achieve it. When you have a dream, then you have something to focus on and work toward, which will guide and motivate every decision you make. The question about a dream is actually about being able to develop a tactical business approach that will lead you to your strategic objective. Having a dream and articulating it are the first steps toward achieving it.

When we launched CST, my partner, Bobby Bradley, and I sat down and discussed *why* we were going to start a company and *what* we wanted the outcome to be. During our conversation, we realized we needed to separate the company's ultimate objective from the outcomes we desired personally. We came to the conclusion that achieving the former would ultimately result in reaching our personal dreams. I asked Bobby, who grew up in a primarily African American neighborhood in North Huntsville, Alabama, "What's your dream?"

She thought about it for a minute and said, "If we can get the company's value to a significant level where we could sell it and become financially free, I'd like to, somehow, give back to my people." She was referring to the young people who were growing up in her childhood neighborhood.

That dream motivated her all the way to our successful liquidity event. Why? Because it was bigger than her. Focusing on working hard so you can give back and help others can diminish your career stress and ease the challenges associated with growing a company. Having a personal dream is a critical success principle. The applicable pearl here is:

> "Having a dream is what keeps you alive.
> Overcoming the challenges makes life worth living."
> – MARY TYLER MOORE

So, as you are thinking about launching your business and continuing to grow it, take some time to ask yourself: "What would I do if I were financially free? What's my dream?"

Dream-building Sessions

What I call "dream-building sessions" provide the perfect opportunity to develop an understanding of both your own personal dream and those of the people around you. As with the human element strategy, which I will discuss next, there is a priceless benefit to holding these sessions regularly. And it's easy to do.

It starts with having a dream yourself before holding a session with someone else, of course. But, as a business leader, there will be numerous opportunities to hold dream-building sessions. Opportunities can be as simple or basic as asking a recruit what their dream is during an interview (which I discuss in greater detail in the section about hiring in Part Three) or as complicated as having a facilitator at your annual leadership team off-site event lead a session in which each team member shares their dream with their colleagues.

As a business leader, the most effective and valuable dream-building session is a one-on-one lunch or coffee break with an emerging employee. Inviting someone like that for a private discussion creates in them a feeling of gratitude and the person is open to your message. The message here is that this interchange reinforces this employee's understanding that the company's culture is about helping people, especially employees, who will ultimately sustain the positive work environment. So, you simply ask your guest, "What's your dream?" That question changes the essences of the meeting—it's about the other person, and you are also practicing the human element strategy. If they start articulating their career objectives you have to stop them and explain that you are asking them what they would do after having a very successful career and they find themselves financially free.

The valuable outcome from these sessions is subtle. On the surface it creates an interesting dialog and helps the individual get a grip on what they want out of life. But the underlying value is in the fact that the individual (subconsciously or consciously) realizes that you care about them, which draws them to you. A huge positive outcome is that it can secure your workforce, who will tell everyone they know what a great place your company is to work.

Another great opportunity for a dream-building session is at one of your weekly leadership team staff meetings. Normally staff meetings are operational in nature. During our successful growth periods at CST, we structured one of each month's four weekly staff meetings to purposely have it strategically focused. We would start by having our CFO, Kevin Webber, brief us on how close we were at that point to meeting our annual revenue goals. We would then go around the room asking the team members individually to revisit their dreams with us, which led to a lively discussion resulting in buy-in from the team on why we were growing our company. It's important to hold these dream session staff meetings in the virtual environment we've mentioned earlier. These virtual meetings are structured similarly to in-person ones, with the CFO opening the meeting with the financial status. Then, assuming the virtual application provides screenshots of the attendees, you replicate the dream-building strategy and ask the attendees one-by-one to share their dream.

So, the importance of dream-building sessions is multifaceted. Through them, you can vet people based on their answer. In a group it has the effect of bringing a team together and ultimately it has a motivating effect and creates an opportunity to revisit why you're doing what you do. However, there could be a negative side to this dream-building session concept that can be turned into a positive. Sometimes a smart technology savvy individual can leak their way onto a leadership team, and they can sometimes be all about *their* knowledge and *their* importance and think this dream stuff is a bunch of hoopla. They suffer from having what we coined "ingrown eyeballs"—they only care about what the company can do for them.

In our experience, these people were purged or left the company on their own because they just couldn't stand the positive culture. That was the positive outcome I mentioned earlier; the dream session helped identify problem people before they became a problem. And because we had our personal dreams in place and were clear about them, we didn't let anyone slow us down or steal our dream.

On a personal note, my dream has changed over time even though it shares the theme of wanting to help people. My goal at CST was to help as many people as I could to achieve and realize their own dreams. As it became obvious that CST was having success and we would reach our liquidity objective, my dream migrated to something closer to my partner's, which was wanting to give back. In my case, though, it was to share with young business owners and entrepreneurs what my partner and I had learned about growing and building a successful technology company. That is my dream even today and that is what I hope to accomplish with this book and my consulting activity.

The Human Element

I use the phrase *the human element strategy* to mean the following: At every turn and in every decision we make, we are dealing with people—be they our clients, customers, family, or employees. Applying the human element strategy to every decision we make involves never losing focus of how that decision will influence those around us. So, we need to make all our decisions keeping in mind the needs, desires, and goals of those people we're engaging, while, at the same time, we try to image what's on their minds. The applicable pearl is below, with my addition in parenthesis:

> "If you help enough people (with a dream) get what they want, you get what you want."
> – ZIG ZIGLAR

When we apply the human element strategy successfully, we can set ourselves apart—professionally and personally—because people are naturally drawn to people who care about them. I have seen this time and time again and I know it works.

The essence of this strategy is to listen closely during each interaction we have, and "climb inside the head" of whomever we're speaking with, looking directly into their eyes (when we can), to truly develop an understanding of where they're coming from and what they need. When we do this, we can successfully meet that need—be it a product, a contract opportunity, or a potential employment engagement—and the person knows that they were heard and that we are sincerely focused on helping them. This, in essence, is applying the human element strategy.

Applying the Human Element Strategy

This principle is not new. The whole idea goes back for millennia; in fact, it's biblical. Giving, sharing, and caring for other human beings are basic practices necessary to achieve a fulfilled life. So why not internalize the idea and apply it every day in your business?

In researching the human element concept, I discovered other industry leaders commenting on the subject. In an article in *Entrepreneur* magazine, Zach Ferres, CEO of Coplex, wrote that, "Every part of your business boils down to people. And by understanding the human element, you'll be more profitable, lead more effectively, create brand loyalty, close more deals and do better work."

The human element strategy is critical, even in today's fast-paced and high-tech world. If more business owners and leaders practiced it, I believe they would be more successful and have greater trust and engagement with their businesses and among their employees. I know this is true because I lived it in the nineties and continue to practice it today—it is indeed a timeless and proven-effective principle.

Many of us in the government contracting world can get so focused on the business at hand that we forget the value of positively interacting with the people around us on a basic human level. If we can keep the human element at the forefront of our minds, it will guide us as we make each of the tactical and strategic decisions we face. When we lose sight of the human element, we can become derailed from our ultimate corporate objectives.

Applying the Human Element
Strategy Starts with You

Successfully applying the human element in life and in our businesses starts with those of us in leadership or ownership positions. This is the only way to ensure that it becomes widely practiced at every level of our business. So that requires slowing down for a moment and finding a quiet place and calmly looking inside yourself and asking:

- Who am I?
- What am I doing here?
- What am I trying to accomplish in my life?"

In answering these questions, you will likely begin to envision and visualize how many people are in your life and you'll begin to think about how they were drawn to you. The answer is that the people who are close to us and who are part of our lives likely got there because we helped them, cared for them, shared with them, and loved them. What happened in these cases is that we were applying the human element, maybe without realizing it. But our caring and focusing on them drew them to us because we had been overlaying the human element over time in our engagements with them.

Leadership Team

It is my very strong belief that understanding the positive impact of applying the human element in our business dealings and our personal lives is the only way we can successfully share and teach others to apply this concept in their lives, particularly in the case of sharing it with our business leadership teams and ultimately our entire business workforce. Below are a few ways you can simply and easily apply the human element strategy in your day-to-day activities with your leadership team.

- Instead of kicking off your Monday morning staff meeting by launching immediately into business and problem issues, consider opening with, "Hey, everybody, I hope you had an enjoyable weekend and I'm glad you are here safely. Also, before we get started, who had a positive weekend event they'd like to share with us?"

    Having been around a while, I've witnessed "old school management thinking" which might reject this suggestion, but the current workforce appreciates this kind of positive culture, which I believe creates trust and loyalty and continues to enhance a culture of caring and sincerity.

- During a leadership team member's annual performance review session, start with something like, "Hey, I know this is a planned annual performance review, but let's start by looking over your self-evaluation document and discussing how you feel about your job. Rest assured, we want to really know how you feel about it and if it's not satisfying your personal career objectives, let's see what other positions we have that you could get excited about."

    This is an example of how applying the human element creates a positive and collaborative workplace environment. Taking a moment to apply the human element strategy to an annual review event reminds the employee in front of you that they are more than just performing a role in your company. It results in their feeling valued and cared about and will make them want to stay with your company.

These examples go on and on. And you'll notice that these are simple and easy things to do, but they can make a huge difference. The point is that it's easy to get caught up in what's on our minds and forget that at every turn we have an opportunity to engage our leadership team members by genuinely caring about them and continually leaving them with a lasting positive impression. If you consistently practice overlaying every encounter with the human element strategy, you will have a leadership team who likes you, feels empowered by you, and who will continually support your objectives.

Customers, Associates, and Digital Examples

The opportunities to apply the human element truly exist at every turn, with everyone you interact with, and even exist when you can't be face-to-face. Below are some more examples of ways you can apply the human element strategy with your customers, associates, and digitally.

- You have just walked into your customer's office for a contract status discussion. Before launching into the contract dialog, you open with something that references an earlier discussion you had. You open the dialog with something like: "The last time we were together you mentioned that you and your wife were going on vacation. How was it?"

- You're meeting with a contract team and an associate partnering contractor to discuss pursuing an opportunity together. In this group setting you again have an opportunity to exercise the human element strategy. Before the group goes into a discussion about the current opportunity you open by asking the attendees to share their previous successful experiences with opportunity pursuits relative to proposal approaches and theme building. You get them talking and you listen.

- Imagine you are about to have a recurring federal government DoD customer monthly status meeting on a project. Everyone is sitting around a conference table and the meeting is about to begin. You say, "Well, here we are again together to discuss how our project is doing and its status. But today I'd like to open the meeting by stating how appreciative we are to have you as a customer. This work is so important, and we appreciate your funding that is so effectively supporting our men and women on active duty." I know you have to pick your moments to do this with customers who may have an attitude and react with a shrug and just want to get on with it, but there will be positive customers whose projects are going well and a comment like that would be appropriate.

- Here is an example of strengthening a contract partnering relationship with a prime or sub-contractor. You are having lunch with these partnering individuals and everyone has just been seated. You open with, "I want to thank you for taking the time today to have lunch with us. You must know how important our relationship is as we continue to work together on these projects and how excited we are to continue this relationship as we pursue future opportunities together." What I'm telling you here is obvious and you may understand it and are even doing it, but I'm emphasizing it because you have to develop an ongoing approach to think about it continually and always prepare to apply it in every engagement; you are becoming a human element practitioner.

- Another opportunity for overlaying the human element is in your email and social media exchanges. When we receive a business-related email, we sometimes are in such a hurry that we just reply with a pointed response. By doing this, though, we miss an opportunity to overlay the response with something like, "Thanks for sending me this message," or "I'm glad to hear from you on this situation." Adding something personal gives us the opportunity to remind the other person that they are important to us. The other important habit to get into is to respond using the name of the person who sent you the message.

Opportunities for practicing the human element strategy will present themselves constantly. You will have to decide if you are going to practice it or not. My genuine hope is that you do because doing so is what will set you apart from your competitors and will keep your workforce and everyone around you positive, motivated, and appreciative.

Outcome Management

In subsequent chapters we will be discussing applying success principles and practices to enhance your business success. Helping you learn how to apply these Pearls of Business in your day to day activity is the focus of this book. A prerequisite for applying these principles starts with understanding that every engagement you enter into must be preceded by an outcome management objective. Researching the phrase *outcome management* yielded the following pearl from IBM:

> "Outcome management is a client-centric model, which puts the needs of the clients first."

In growing CST, Bobby and I never went into a client business development meeting without having done some serious preparation work beforehand. We applied an outcome management strategy prior to any meeting we went into. We would think through the following questions:

- Who is this client?
- What is their perception of us?
- What is their mission?
- What is our understanding of their current challenges?
- What do we offer that can be adapted to optimally support them?

We practiced this outcome management technique with every engagement, including meetings with existing customers and during our staff meetings. Because we had thought beforehand about the outcome we wanted, the resulting conversations and discussions would inevitably lead to positive results. In other words, we imaged the outcome we wanted going in, prepared well for the meeting, and kept that image in our minds, which guided the discussion. We would frequently reach a point near the end of a sales meeting to ask a closing question. We learned to apply a Columbo tactic.

We would stand, smile, thank the prospective client for their time, move toward the door, then turn and ask something like, "By the way, George, when we come back next week for a follow-up, should we meet with you and your COO or just you?" This closing question is critical in that it can't be answered with a simple yes or no. By asking about the future, you're showing that you're planning for it and giving the person you're engaging with the opportunity to commit to meeting with you again. So, creating this outcome management environment led to closing deals and the ultimate successful growth of our company.

Soon after the launch of CST, we had the great privilege of meeting with Larry Womack, business consultant and author of the book *Outcome Management*. That meeting and his book provided us with priceless insight and advice. He gave us one of the greatest pearls.

> "Outcome management is determining a desired outcome and managing toward it.
> It is managing *from* the future instead of *for* it."
> – LARRY WOMACK

He shared with us that, "Managing effective outcomes requires expectations of leaders, managers, and workers and a demand for adherence to those expectations from everyone." Womack states in his book that the guiding principle for leaders in an outcome management environment is to, "Dream before you think, think before you plan, and plan before you act, and that it demands a stamina of spirit, courage of conviction, and leadership mettle." In other words, outcome management is accomplished successfully in an organization throughout the entire operational team; the owners and leadership team pass it down and they all accomplish it by practicing it daily.

What Larry is sharing with us is that having outcome management in mind continually affects every engagement during day-to-day operations. I can attest to its importance and effectiveness. The more you practice it, the more it becomes central to every business encounter, both internally and externally.

Outcome Management Anecdotes

An example of applying the outcome management strategy affected me personally in a positive way relative to my career. While I was still supporting the Ballistic Missile Defense Systems Command in the early 1970s at Computer Sciences Corporation (CSC) in Huntsville, Alabama, one of my CSC coworkers who had accepted a job with Advanced Technology, Inc. (ATI) approached me with a suggestion that I should consider interviewing with ATI because they were looking for someone to launch a branch office in Huntsville.

I was contacted and invited to meet with ATI's leadership team in their Reston, Virginia, headquarters to discuss my interest. Here was my outcome management thought at the time: I decided not to just show up at this meeting and wing the discussion. I thought through what their agenda might be and what their expectations were. I did some homework on what it would take to launch their branch office. I contacted several office complexes for office space costs and even investigated phone, copier, and other overhead costs, including a receptionist.

I drafted a briefing in preparation for my interview. When I arrived, I was invited into the main conference room and the ATI president and the entire leadership team were there, including my colleague. Following introductions, I opened my comments with my background and experience then reached down and opened my briefcase and pulled out the copies of the briefing and acknowledged they were looking for someone to open an office in Huntsville for them.

I said I had thought through what I felt might be required to accomplish that, passed around the presentation, and briefed it. After I answered a few questions from the group, the president asked me to step out of the room for a few minutes. In a relatively short time, they invited me back into the conference room and offered me the job on the spot. I had imaged the outcome I wanted and prepared my remarks to give the ATI leaders what I actually thought it would take to open a branch office successfully. I acted like I had the job, took the necessary steps to ensure I would get it, and it worked.

Another vivid personal example of an outcome management application came to me during a proposal activity I was leading at ATI following the tragic loss of NASA's Shuttle Challenger during its launch in the mid-1980s. The Marshall Space Flight Center (MSFC) was responsible for all of NASA's propulsion systems design and development and it took full responsibility for the success and possible failure of every shuttle launch. As a result, the entire MSFC staff and personnel were devastated by the Challenger loss and were, for a while, in a state of depression.

Following the accident, NASA's MSFC leadership made a decision to assure that such an event would never happen again, and they launched a program to form a new Safety, Reliability, Maintainability & Quality Assurance (SRM&QA) Program. The contracts office released a Request for Proposal (RFP) solicitation to find and award a qualified contractor to fulfill and support MSFC's SRM&QA requirements.

ATI decided to compete for the contract, and I was asked to lead the proposal effort from our Huntsville office. Those of us who were close to NASA during this time were also devastated by the accident. As I put the proposal team together it became important to me that the writers and responders to the RFP had a grasp of both the current state of mind of MSFC in general, but also that of the proposal evaluators, specifically. I knew they would be looking for a contractor who understood their current state of mind and the depth of their commitment to assure that another failure of that magnitude would never happen again, and I wanted to make sure my team understood that, too.

In order to gain a clear picture of this outcome management anecdote, I need to share with you something I had experienced during the early days of NASA's Shuttle Program, prior to the loss of the Challenger. In 1981, the US Space and Rocket Center's (USSRC) IMAX Dome Theater was featuring a powerful documentary, *Hail Columbia,* about the first flight of the Space Shuttle Program (STS1). When I watched it earlier, I had an enormous feeling of pride and excitement for our future space exploration.

So, back to the proposal effort. I realized that we had a once-in-a-lifetime opportunity to help the devastated MSFC staff get their excitement back. The next morning when the proposal team arrived, I sat everyone down and said, "Folks, we're going over to the USSRC's Dome Theater and we're going to watch the movie *Hail Columbia* so you can personally feel the pride and excitement this NASA team had after the first successful shuttle flight." I said that the NASA proposal evaluators would need to feel that we understood what they had experienced and that if they selected us, we were going to take them back there.

When we arrived back from the movie and the writing commenced, our proposal accomplished the outcome I was looking for. We were awarded the contract.

Applying the Pearl

An important commitment to incorporating this outcome management strategy into your operation is to, from time to time, create opportunities to hold outcome management exercise sessions. The most effective exercise is to make a list of some settings where you and your team image situations and then create some mock engagements with colleagues and practice the meeting outcome technique. An effective approach is to have a pre-practice session discussion and set up a staff meeting scenario so you can think through how and when to insert the outcome management technique. Just setting up the scenario supports the leadership team's internalizing the technique.

Outcome management must be an ongoing activity and state of mind. As a leader and company principal you internalize it first, pass it down to your leadership team, encourage them to pass it down, and you continually protect it from wavering. Applying the strategy takes some practice. Below you will find some ways to practice imaging, which will, with a little bit of work, become second nature to you.

- Take a few minutes to act out some scenarios you might find your-self in and practice how to achieve the desired outcome. Say you have a meeting with a big client about your new product or service. What is the desired goal and outcome from that meeting? How will you achieve that outcome using imaging?

- Before each meeting or engagement, meet briefly with your leader-ship team. Practice in real-time what you put in place in the above strategy. Ask them what they expect, or image, will happen during the meeting and ask them what they anticipate the outcome will be.

- Just think for a moment about what would happen to your business if every time you went into a business development engagement, a staff meeting, or a board meeting you imaged the outcome you wanted and it actually happened. Where could that take you?

The applicable pearl here is:

> "Hold an image of the life you want,
> and that image will become fact."
> – NORMAN VINCENT PEALE

My adaptation of it is:

> "Hold an image of the *outcome* you want,
> and that image will become fact."

Getting Inside
People's Heads

A n important aspect of overlaying the human element in every engagement, in having a dream, and in exercising outcome management includes developing the skill to look at and listen carefully to what the person you are engaging with needs and wants and, most importantly, how they view you. Your first reaction to that statement may be, "Why do I care what that person is thinking about me?" The reason it's important is captured by the following pearl:

> "You only have one chance to make
> a good first impression!"
> – DAN PEÑA

If your approach to business, and life, for that matter, is focused on helping other people get what they want, then learning this technique is vital to your success. Why? People are generally perceptive and can tell what your motives are. Whoever best reads the other person's needs and articulates how they can help them get it, will win the engagement's objective.

I've been asked many times, "How do you really get inside someone else's head?" First, since you have bought this book and are starting or running a business or leading a business organization, you are probably an entrepreneur and hopefully have a positive self-image. The reason that's important is that when you get inside the head of another person and look back at yourself, *you* must like what you see. The ultimate objective once you've gained that insight is so that you can formulate, in real time, what that person is struggling with and determine what they need.

The other critical component of this approach to interfacing with people is that you have taken the time to investigate who they are—their name, title, business offerings, and/or their areas of interest. During the early part of the interchange you have asked questions, listened more than talked, and gained enough insight into the other person to address how you could help them, which may lead to a formal relationship.

This approach works successfully if your motive is honestly about helping the other person. Keep in mind that a possible perception of this technique could conclude that it's manipulative. It's not if, again, the objective leads to a positive and supportive outcome. Understanding and applying this approach to every personal engagement leads to you building a reputation as a person who is seriously able to help other people get what they want and need.

Applying the Pearl

An anecdote on this subject comes from CST's mid-course growth period. We had been approached by an earlier colleague of mine, Randy Cash, who said that he and some of his associates wanted to join CST. We invited him to join us for lunch so we could discuss the possibilities. I recall that Bobby and I had a conversation before this engagement and talked through the things I've been sharing with you in this "Getting Inside People's Heads" chapter including: What do we know about Randy's role in his current job position? What is his perception of us? Who are his colleagues? What are their expectations? What is their time-frame objective for joining CST?

Because we had taken the time to think through these questions and had some educated insight into Randy's objectives and expectations, the outcome of the luncheon meeting was outstanding and in fact became a CST milestone. Randy and his team joined us and ultimately led us to becoming an information technology powerhouse, which led us to our successful liquidity event. We were able to figure out what Randy needed, determine how we could help him, and make decisions that were mutually beneficial to everyone involved.

The SMART Approach

A s the close to Part One, I am going to discuss how to be SMART about overlaying the human element, the importance of having a dream, and applying outcome management onto everyday operations and the activity of running your company. There is a SMART approach to doing that successfully as follows:

S – Strategic thinking fundamentally leads to business success. It starts with developing a sound business plan that contains **strategies** associated with why you are building this business and, at a high level, where you are going with it. The other strategic thinking activity takes place stepwise and is accomplished by making ongoing focused strategic decisions day-to-day.

M – Motivate your leadership team and gain their buy-in to the current year's goals while keeping in mind the ultimate business liquidity objective. A motivated leadership team that trusts one another will lead to collaborative successful outcomes. The inspired leadership team will **mobilize** and move the company forward.

A – Articulate in clear and unmistakable terms your personal dreams and protect your company culture through assuring your founders and leadership team members have positive mental **attitudes** and all your "why's" are clearly in mind and visited frequently.

R – Resilient companies and their leadership teams adapt their products and solutions as markets evolve and these adaptations continue to respond to customers' **real** needs. The adaptations result in recognizable solutions your market sectors continue to seek.

T – Transformation suggests agility. That we understand the problem and are willing to introduce disruptive **technological** products and services to our markets. Understanding this leads to unique solutions assuring our government customers are fulfilling their missions and protecting our way of life, so our pursuit of happiness is intact through our successful government contract performance.

Strategic Thinking

Over time, the industry norm is for company founders to develop an initial long-term strategic plan in the early going right after the business plan is drafted. This plan lays out the operational strategy that will lead to achieving the company's ultimate objective at liquidity. The other strategic thinking approaches are the ongoing, stepwise, operational steps that must be accomplished day-to-day by making decisions that support the company's overall strategic direction.

The prerequisite to successfully executing strategically is continually applying the human element strategy, understanding the importance of having a dream, and using outcome management strategies on all operational activity and decisions.

Motivating and Mobilizing

We have all heard and believe that our most valuable business assets are our people. Given that, your company's successes depend on organizing, motivating, and mobilizing all your employees, including your leadership teams. This is accomplished initially by drafting an effective business plan and executing its guidance early and consistently (which I discuss in greater detail in Part Two).

Motivating your leadership team begins with applying the guidance discussed earlier on the topics of the human element, the importance of dreams, and outcome management. If your leadership team understands and believes working with your company will result in their accomplishing their career goals and ultimate dreams, then they will surely join hands with you and the other team members and run.

Given you have successfully accomplished the above, the related and most critical next objective is mobilization. That starts by launching your new fiscal year with an annual kickoff meeting (discussed in Part Three). The critical agenda items for this event include discussing the new business development focus and pursuits, revisiting the company's ultimate liquidity objective, and reemphasizing that accomplishing that will result in everyone reaching their life objectives and individual dreams.

Articulating Objectives and Positive Attitudes

Frequently and clearly articulating your company's ultimate liquidity objective and personal dream is an important early discussion practice during individual engagements and in selected staff meetings. But beyond that, emphasizing the importance of your leadership team having positive mental attitudes is one of the key attributes your business must have in order to attract the right people to your company and to assure successful growth.

As a business leader with leadership team members reporting to you, it is imperative that you surround yourself with people with positive outlooks. It only takes one negative thinker in a group or team to drag everyone down. You must frequently emphasize the importance of having positive outlooks and hold appropriate training sessions on the subject.

Resilience and Real Customer Needs

Launching and successfully growing a federal government support contracting company requires constantly assessing the government's current budgets and future program projections. Your company's resilience and survival are dependent on your performing these continual assessments.

Accomplishing successful assessment of the government's budgets and future program projections draws attention to your current contracts' longevities and continuations and brings you face-to-face with the validity of your current contract base solutions. Assessing your future focus brings attention to the need to refine your annual business development projections. This results in clarifying your current customers' needs, which may be evolving, and leads to jointly assessing those needs and updating those contracts' scopes of work.

The reason this is important to resilience is that leading and growing a business requires constant assessment of the issues at hand and the current challenging situations. Assessing these challenges supports resilience but doing so can be all-consuming, which makes performing these future market assessments hard to get to given your tactical obligations. However, this is necessary work that must be done.

Transformation via Technological Innovation

Current business guidance and industry focus frequently discusses offering innovative and disruptive products and services. I have to admit that the first impact on me of the term *disruptive* was negative. But the more I faced the onslaught of this concept the closer I came to internalizing it. Now it has become an integral component of my counseling. Why?

Disruptive technology has become a focus because of both technological advances and the evolving workforce. An example of technological advancement is artificial intelligence (AI). The truth is that AI solutions are beginning to accomplish, for the government, what we used to be contracted to perform. So, for this example there is a real need for us to learn how to apply AI approaches to our future customer solutions' development. AI is just one concept that is transforming our future government business environment. Innovation is constantly emphasized in the government's ever-increasing requests for information (RFI) and requests for proposal (RFP) solicitations. Tactically applying innovative **technological** applications are **transforming** the future government business environment. So, ready or not, transformation and technological innovation are upon us and understanding their impact on your businesses and how the evolving workforce will respond to them will separate you from the competition.

> "The more time you spend contemplating what you should have done... you lose valuable time planning what you can and will do."
> – LIL WAYNE

Keep in mind the **SMART** approach to growing your company as you read the rest of the book, which will provide you with ways to apply these strategies as you launch your company, refine your operating principles and business processes, stabilize and anchor your operation, and accelerate your growth while optimizing your company's value moving toward a successful liquidity event.

PART TWO

Launch Point

Given that you are, in fact, starting a business, your motivation should be positive. Your decision to start and build a business should move you toward your dream and not away from working for someone else in frustration. You will quickly learn that when you own a business or you are a principle of an existing one, you will always be working for everybody else: your employees, your banker, your attorney, your CPA, and many others. All of this working for other people leads to the theme and genesis of *The Pearls of Business*.

So, starting a business is a leap of faith. It begins with a dream which fuels the business idea. Then the business plan is born, and the company launches with early customers. Initial employees join you, leading to insurance, vacation, and other benefit costs. Financing and a bank line of credit become necessary. You are now in business and the realization that you are working during the day for clients and running the business at night sets in.

"Success doesn't happen overnight.
Keep your eye on the prize and don't look back."
– ERIN ANDREWS

An important ingredient in launching a business is a clearly defined personal dream, as discussed in Part One. I will remind you that I am not referring to the business goals or objectives. Your dream fuels the business goals and objectives and ultimately pulls you through whatever obstacles confront you and your leadership team, employees, and your family as well. It is extremely important for you and the emerging leadership team to develop their own clearly defined personal dreams, again not company goals or objectives. In this part of the book we will look at the issues you will initially face as you launch your company.

Solidifying the Business Idea

You've made the decision to launch your own business. But now is the time to move from that decision into solidifying your idea. Solidifying your business idea involves doing research on it so that you can assess the need, identify who your competitors are, evaluate the risk, assess your financing needs, determine how solid the market is that you are pursuing, and find out if there are some existing business models for this market. This early activity will provide important information that will be included in your business plan. What follows is an explanation of what we went through at CST during this phase as we followed these steps to solidify our business idea.

> "Your business idea is solidified by discovering that other businesses are doing it, but your research shows they are only dealing with current issues and their version of your idea is not innovative and future focused."
> – JAY NEWKIRK

Assessing the Need

At this early stage at CST my partner and I knew the Systems Engineering and Technical Assistance (SETA) and Information Technology (IT) markets were exploding. Our primary target client base was the National Aeronautics and Space Administration's (NASA) Marshall Space Flight Center (MSFC) and the US Army Missile Command (MICOM) located in Huntsville, Alabama. The need was clear because in the early 1990s desktop computing was maturing, the internet was in its early development stage, and data systems were evolving rapidly. We knew that these important government agencies were under great pressure to build and support data systems that provided rapidly accessible engineering and information solutions that supported their urgent mission objectives.

Identifying the Competition

At the point my partner and I had decided to launch our business we were both deeply engaged in the market we were about to launch into. I was working for a professional services company engaged in supporting our target market, and my partner was a government employee. As a result, we were in meetings and were engaged with existing potential partnering companies.

> "Competition is always a good thing.
> It forces us to do our best . . ."
> – NANCY PEARCY

We knew that our competitors were numerous and, to some degree, ominous. But we also realized that we were in a vibrant market sector so we would have to somehow distinguish ourselves and find a niche. The emerging IT market sector became our focus and was attracting all the major aerospace companies supporting our primary target client base. Having worked for many years with and for some of these companies, we knew their IT market focus was real.

Evaluating Risk

As you contemplate launching a business there is an obvious excitement and determination to move ahead and launch. A somewhat uncomfortable aspect of accomplishing it successfully is looking closely at the risks of doing it. Risk assessment can include a wide range of topics including: your current financial situation, the current stability of your target market, and the strength of your competitor base.

In CST's early risk assessment we focused on whether we could actually compete with the large prime contractors who were establishing IT divisions and data systems initiatives. Our assessment concluded that the large companies who were supporting our target government programs tended to be secure in their customer relationships and were, to some degree, sluggish in making changes and innovation. Our conclusions and risk mitigation included that the fact that we were a small company with reduced overhead optimized our ability to respond rapidly to our customers' evolving requirements.

Assessing Financing Needs

At this early phase of launching CST we did follow the then-current guidance for launching a business and we developed our initial business plan. An important segment of the business plan was the Financial Section. In the case of assessing our financing needs we went into our business plan and looked at our three- to five-year projections and ran "what-if analyses" and trade-off studies to determine what our possible staff requirements would be based on revenue projections. We then assessed the resulting infrastructure investment requirements. These analyses were very much driven by our projected revenue growth objectives.

Market Solidity

The approach to assessing the solidity of your chosen market sector will vary significantly in both the commercial and government markets. You will need to assess the current stability of the economy in general and specifically your market area. This assessment needs to include reaching out to potential customers and other business leaders currently supporting your target customers and gaining their perspective on your market sector pursuit.

In the case of our CST market solidity assessment, we had been working in this market for years supporting other people and we knew the IT market was growing rapidly inside the federal market sector. Our challenge in launching our own business was to figure out how we would compete with a number of very large competitors beginning to expand their IT support capability. It was at that moment that we developed our competitive approach, which basically took into account that we were small and flexible thus enabling us to respond quickly and affordably while also being able to adapt our IT and data systems knowledge and solutions to fit the customers' requirements. That decision ultimately led to our byline: "Our Mission is You."

Existing Business Models

There were very defining business models evolving in the IT market when we were launching CST. So, your assessment of the market solidity should reveal the maturity of your chosen target market and provide some insight into business models that may become part of your ultimate business model application. At CST we were developing a strategy for attracting some of our early leadership team members from larger companies who were developing their IT strategy and organizations. These individuals would provide us with insight into these larger competitors' strategies and processes which would provide us with insight into some existing business models.

We had made the decision at that point to grow a professional services company, which was basically the business models of the IT divisions of the large aerospace companies we were familiar with and, in some cases, had come from and were planning to replicate. What we learned was that our strength was in our size and agility and ability to respond quickly and personally. That is the benefit of learning about these existing business models of larger companies—we could figure out what they weren't able to do and poise ourselves to deliver the solution.

A Word of Caution

The following anecdote speaks to the importance of thoroughly researching your idea to ensure that it is viable, at every aspect of your business strategy, whether it is at the start-up phase or in an expansion mode. This situation came to CST after we had been in business for a while, but the lesson learned about diversifying prematurely is important for you as you are in the early planning stage. Keep in mind as you read this that CST was focused on the expanding IT and data systems market sectors.

About five years into CST's operation, two of our engineers approached us with an idea for a product in the poultry industry breeder market for weighing top-of-the-food-chain genetically engineered breeder eggs. We investigated the product idea and found little or no competition and substantiated the industry need. We ran computer searches on the number of breeders to further substantiate the market strength and ultimately launched the project. Two years and $250,000 later, we realized the number of prime breeders who could use the product in the U.S. was nine. The number we saw in the research was worldwide and most were outside our ability to market.

As you can see, there is a need to be diligent in the business concept analysis and not be so passionate about an idea that you miss the clues to rethink expanding into an alien market.

> "Diversification is a good thing.
> Diversifying too early is not."
> – JAY NEWKIRK

The other important lesson learned is to stay focused on your core capability and diversify only after you are solidly established in your focused target market.

Gaining Buy-in from Spouse, Friends, and Family

As you are contemplating launching your own business, gaining buy-in from the family is absolutely necessary. One of the key pearls that is applicable in numerous situations, but especially at this point, is that:

> "It's easier to run with a hundred than drag one."
> – DEXTER YAGER

This couldn't be more valid than in the family buying into your business launch, desire, and objective. Following is an anecdote that addresses this and explains why this is a critical step in launching your business.

Before my partner and I launched CST, we spent a number of years building a multilevel business together. In that business we were constantly recruiting people to join us so we could help them likewise build a business for themselves. One evening we were visiting a couple in their home and sharing the multilevel business concept with them. As always, we came to a point in the dialog where we asked them about their dreams. In this case, the wife, in a very animated way, excitedly unfolded a sequence of things she had always imaged doing or having. But what happened next had a huge impact on both my partner and me.

When the wife finished sharing all of her wants and dreams, her husband turned toward her with a frown and said, "That's not your dream." He then immediately moved away from us and sat down in a corner chair and went into a near fetal position. We spent a few more minutes encouraging the wife, but as we left their home my partner's eyes met mine. We both knew that we would not be able to help this couple because, if we did, we'd be dragging the husband, which could ultimately affect their marriage. This is a striking example about the above pearl's point about "dragging one."

This is an exhaustive example of the importance of gaining spousal buy-in on the plan to launch a business. Business is hard enough when everyone is holding hands and running, but dragging a spouse or family member makes success nearly impossible.

Applying the Pearl

The tendency at the business launch point is for you, as the founder, to ask friends, family, and associates their opinion about your idea, which may result in your first lesson in dealing with rejection. If you believe a widely held theory called the "80/20 Rule" then you know that 80 percent of the people on the planet and surrounding you at the moment are not positive or motivated to think independently about any part of their lives. They believe that there is security in numbers and generally tend to blame others for their circumstances and make excuses at every turn. So when you ask people close to you about your business idea, prepare to listen but don't react or even respond, just smile. I encourage you to constantly keep in mind this pearl:

"Don't react to **what** people say,
react to **why** they said it."
– JAY NEWKIRK

If people are negative and discouraging, relax and focus on who they are and *why* they would react that way. Your calmness is disarming, and the silence works in your favor. What you do at this point is get inside the other person's head and look back at yourself and imagine what they are seeing and thinking, which we discussed in Part One. Remember, you're practicing overlaying the human element onto all of your interactions, with everyone. As stated earlier, when you focus on that, you'll win.

So, getting inside the head of the family member you are engaged with will give you insight into their response. Your spouse might be thinking about losing the security you have in your current job if you set out on your own. Your siblings might be thinking that you are going to launch this business and succeed and make them look bad. Your parents might worry about you failing or getting hurt somehow. The application of this pearl is responding to *why* they say something. For example, your spouse might ask about losing the security of your present job. It is important to think through why your spouse is saying something like that, which may be out of caring and concern rather than criticism or not being supportive. Given that their response is out of concern, we can feel less defensive and be more able to respond positively. A pearl to contemplate in this situation is:

> "Security in your work has nothing to do
> with the company you work for or its size,
> it has everything to do with your performance."
> – JAY NEWKIRK

So, you just quote the pearl and remind your spouse that you have done very well over the years with promotions and salary increases all due to your performance. But herein lies an important hint about being mature and controlling your own enthusiasm in the case you are at first met with resistance by someone close to you.

You should not start talking about your idea with anyone outside your immediate support group until you have analyzed your business concept to the point that you are totally convinced that it is a good one and will work, given your passion, persistence, and commitment. Be armed with a response to those types of questions or reactions. Also, here is a good place to remind you about using outcome management. Here's the pearl to help you as you navigate gaining buy-in:

> "Never go into any conversation, sales call, or meeting without a clear image of the desired outcome."
> – LARRY WOMACK

If you master the use of this pearl and continually apply it in every encounter, you will start experiencing measurable success. Also keep in mind this message:

> "The mind moves in the direction of our currently dominant thoughts."
> – EARL NIGHTINGALE

If you believe this and enter into every conversation with the outcome you want in mind, more often than not you will get the desired result. Remember, the objective of the book is for you to understand the pearls for what they are and apply them at every opportune moment.

Develop Vision and Mission Statements

As you contemplate launching your own business and initiate the activity, you will need to develop both a vision for the company and its mission. This is particularly important as you develop your initial business plan because the vision and mission statements are the company's foundation.

The vision statement is strategic and long-term, while the mission statement is tactical and short-term. Following is some clarifying information that will help you create or rework these important company founding statements. A well-thought-through mission statement can lead to shaping your business plan, while your vision statement is the foundation for your business strategy. A pearl to keep in mind is:

> "Your 'why' is **what you believe**. Your vision is **where you're going**. Your mission **is how you'll get there**."
> – KATE DE JONG

In the case of our early CST days, we did have a vision and a mission. The vision was to build a professional government support services company and reach $100M revenue level in ten years and sell it. The mission was to become an excellent government-recognized small disadvantaged and 8a certified business, which would provide early growth success. An example of a strong vision statement is by Microsoft: "Empower people through great software anytime, anyplace, and on any device." As you create your vision statement, keep in mind that it:

- Focuses on the future
- Is the source of inspiration and motivation
- Captures the future of your organization and the industry
- Expresses how your organization hopes to affect change

Mission Statement

Now that you've got your vision statement, work on your mission statement, which:

- Concentrates on the present
- Defines your customer
- Alludes to critical processes
- Quantifies desired levels of performance

I encourage you to create and/or revisit your vision and mission statements and make sure they are structured as we've discussed. Having well-structured mission and vision statements and keeping them in mind will enable you to accurately and succinctly respond to the questions, "What does your company do?" and "Where is it going?"

Being able to respond quickly and succinctly to what you do and where you are going makes an immediate positive impression on the person who posed the question. You have probably experienced this yourself. When someone you have asked these questions hesitates and struggles answering clearly and responsively, you subconsciously or even consciously question their company's strength. Don't fall into that trap!

Developing a Comprehensive Business Plan

eveloping a well-thought-through initial business plan (BP) is an important early activity when launching your new business. Over time there have been differences of opinion about the value and importance of developing a detailed BP document early. The controversy has come from a tendency for the business plan to be shelved after its creation and not looked at and revisited or used for guidance as the business evolves.

It has been my strong guidance and recommendation that a business plan be thought through and drafted early in your company's launch and that it should, in fact, be revisited and updated often. I also recommend reading *Your First Business Plan* by Joseph Covello and Brian Hazelgren. After reviewing the book, create a series of bulleted slides for each section of a standard business plan, which I have outlined below. By way of clarification, this PowerPoint–type presentation is designed to provide you with a document that summarizes your thoughts on every business plan topic and section of your ultimate plan. It is the outline of what you plan to write about in the ultimate plan document.

In my preparation for discussing the importance of the early creation of an initial business plan, I researched the current counseling on business plan development. While the above reference to *Your First Business Plan* is still valid, I found extensive current articles and advice on the subject, all having their slant on the content and its order. I am including my advice on this subject below, but I encourage you to research the subject and decide what advice and guidance is best for you. The importance of developing a sound and well-thought-out business plan is substantiated by one of the master pearls of business:

> "If one does not know to which port one is sailing, no wind is favorable."
> – LUCIUS SENECA

In order for you to understand the importance of this pearl and to internalize it, you need to reflect on when it was first quoted. Lucius Seneca lived in the first century AD in Rome–controlled Spain. To fully understand the significance of his guidance, you need to think about the basis of commerce in Seneca's time. Commerce then was based on moving people and goods on sailing vessels and, of course, always knowing to where they were sailing. The point here is that your business plan contains your ultimate company objective, your insight into the areas of focus, and the three- to five-year revenue and profit projections: *your port!*

Back when we launched CST we did, in fact, develop an initial business plan, but then it sat on a shelf and we didn't refer to it that I can recall. Since CST's liquidity event, I've been counseling business owners and leadership team members and have come to the conclusion that a well-developed business plan created early and reviewed and updated frequently can result in setting you apart from your competition. How?

Because most business owners and leadership team members are reacting day to day on action items, confusing activity with accomplishment. They are not considering how this ongoing activity and the related decisions could be moving them closer to their annual and liquidity objectives. These day-to-day decisions will affect the company's longer-range objectives. Looking back on our early CST days, we consistently did this but from time to time we didn't assess how our market focus was changing. Over time, we ultimately made sure we assessed our target market evolution continually and thought through how to distinguish ourselves from our competition.

In my current work as the VP for Corporate Strategy supporting my son's company, Government Energy Solutions, Inc., I have been asked to review and update the company's original business plan. So, I am in the throes of taking my own advice as I accomplish this task. While my guidance on building the business plan hasn't changed that much, my advice and counselling now have a new focus and intent.

I am totally convinced now that your BP must be a living document, meaning it should not be just created and shelved. Instead, once it's written it should be revisited quarterly at a designated staff meeting. In that meeting the bulleted presentation mentioned earlier should be brought up and displayed and discussed. Also, the BP executive summary should be available as well. During this important quarterly meeting, the areas that need to be updated should be identified to reflect how the company has evolved since the BP's presentation and executive summary were last reviewed. In doing so, these BP elements become, to some degree, the company's roadmap for the current year's progress.

Applying the Pearl

So, it's important to keep in mind Seneca's guidance as you develop your business plan. What follows is my guidance for what the BP's presentation slides you create should initially include. Again, this is my recommendation among many, but it should help you craft your BP as I also provide brief descriptions of what should be included.

Executive Summary: Written last and summarizes the content of the following main body of the business plan sections.

Company Focus, Mission and Vision: Introduces the company's market focus based on its projected capabilities and the principals' past performance. Includes the desired contract business development pursuits including an explanation of the company's initial mission and vision statements.

Present Situation Highlights: A very important high-level description of the current business environment and how it will affect the early growth of the company. Includes a description of the market environment, the company's products and services, the pricing strategy, the customer environment, the management team, and the current availability of financial resources.

Objectives: Includes your understanding of and an overview of the potential customers and how your projected capabilities and solutions can be adapted to continually support your projected customer base.

Management Responsibilities: Presents the company's organizational structure and profiles the leadership team members. The organizational chart should show what elements of the organization each leadership team member will lead initially.

Business Descriptions and Services: Describes in some detail your current and planned capabilities including packaged services solutions and your planned product offerings. If you plan to have suppliers and partners, their descriptions should be included here.

Marketing and Business Development Analysis and Strategy: Presents your marketing and new business development strategy including the market environment and your target markets. Keep in mind that marketing activity supports new business development and sales.

Describe how your marketing effort will support the sales individuals in mapping the company's focused capability, the markets to pursue, and the marketing material needed by the sales team to function successfully.

Operating Plan: Addresses the organizational structure and each leadership team member's area of responsibility. Identifies the lead operations manager and describes the projected growth strategy and strategic competitive objectives.

Financial Information: Includes the company's financial status and the funding resources used to launch the company. Potential investors and early funding sources must be discussed clearly. If there is debt or if bank lines-of-credit have been acquired to fund the company's launch, then the details of the debt repayment and the investors' expected return should also be described.

An important side note is offered here given the worldwide COVID-19 pandemic underway at the time of this writing. There is no time at this point and beyond to be non-specific. There has never been a more important business environment to be clear and focused on your business plan. Given the pandemic and the competitive environment, we now have a "new normal."

Your business plan, if done well, will require you to think through your vision for why you are launching a business, the services or products you plan to introduce, the markets you are going to pursue, the competition you'll be facing, and a description of how you plan to distinguish yourself in your target market.

Again, your business plan must be comprehensive enough and detailed enough in the marketing and business development section to take the place of what we in the past have referred to as a *business roadmap*. For it to be effective as such, it should be presented to and reviewed with your leadership team and updated at least every quarter to assure it is still relevant.

So, your business plan will provide you with objectives and strategies to guide the operations activity and includes your business offering focus. It also describes what markets you will pursue, your management and leadership strategy, and what your objectives are for the company's ultimate liquidity event.

Including discussions on all the topics mentioned above could possibly lead to a twenty- to thirty-page BP document, so it's important as you review your business plan quarterly that you take advantage of having the bulleted presentation available and use it as the primary reference document during these reviewing events along with the executive summary. Using them as the basis for these company status reviews should provide you and your leadership team the insight you need to continue moving forward successfully. As an important side note, you should assign someone to update the actual BP document later as an outcome.

Organizational Structure

I n the business plan discussion above, under "Management Responsibilities and Operating Plan," I mention organizational structure. This is an important topic and I want to expand on it here.

Traditional support services organizational charts are structured as follows: The President and CEO is at the top. That individual has five direct reports including the Chief Operations Officer (COO), the Chief Technology Officer (CTO), Chief Financial Officer (CFO), VP Business & Administration, and VP Business Development. The COO leads the revenue-generating contracts and all the associated Project Managers (PM). The CTO is the advisor to the President, the CEO, and other officers and PMs on technology issues. The CFO leads the finance & accounting and purchasing operations. The VP Business & Administration includes Human Resources, Contracts, Security, and Facilities activity. The VP Business Development includes Sales, Marketing, and Proposal Development and Communications activities. This structure can vary significantly based the founder's organizational concept and some possible Board of Directors' advice. When you are just starting out you normally would not have all these people on board, but you would want to have these functions defined and someone to take on making sure these functional areas are being addressed.

As a business leader you will be familiar with most of these functions but not necessarily Communications. Some of the activities performed in the Communications area have emerged since our CST days. The current

Communications practices include social media presence and activity, branding, partnership development, planning networking events, and coordinating community support activity. In the past, the marketing function performed some of these activities, but there wasn't focus on it. Given the 2020 coronavirus pandemic, the highly competitive government support contracting environment, and the explosive growth of social media and the internet, it has become imperative that a Communications function be identified and fulfilled.

So, let's say you have created your organizational structure and gained buy-in from your founding colleagues and leadership team. It will be very important that you realize that the organizational chart is a guide to your staff's interoperability and is only effective as the interoperable communication is exercised operationally. The applicable pearl is:

> "If an organization is to work effectively,
> the communication should be through the most
> effective channel regardless of the organization chart."
> – TOM PETERS

There are many organizational ideas and structures that have evolved over time. Some advice I received some time ago was to not over-organize early and get stuck in a structure that doesn't work as your company evolves. In any case, you and your founding partners should sit down and develop a structure that best reflects your projected structural needs. If your company is already established and underway with a number of leadership team members, my advice is to discuss it with them and gain buy-in on the final projected organization.

In closing, I want to share with you that my personal organizational structure counseling and advice varies widely based on the client's target market and whether or not it's a service or product focused company. An organizational structure should reflect the founder and senior staff's collective image of how they will work together and communicate effectively and it should clearly separate the administrative support staff functionality from the revenue-generating operational staff.

My final thought, relative to organizational structure during our CST days, is that Bobby I and were constantly motivating our leadership team to optimize their positive focus and to always remember that we were about helping other people get what they want. So, we made sure that all the leadership members kept in mind who they were helping. For example, we made sure that our administrative support staff knew that their customers were the internal revenue-generating operational staff who themselves were focused on the company's contractual customer's *needs* helping them achieve their organizational mission.

Company Location and Corporate Documentation

Many businesses launch from a home office or garage then later move into an office and/or production facility. The decision to start at home is important and needs more than just a cursory evaluation. As you begin thinking about this, two questions you should ask yourself are:

- Can I work out of my house and separate work from family?
- Do my neighborhood and deed have restrictions relative to running a business out of my home?

If the answers are in favor of starting at home, then by all means do so. It is important to involve your family members in the decision so they understand the ground rules about not disturbing you during work hours. Another important factor is forward pricing. Pricing for your product or service needs to be calculated as though you have outside facility overhead. As you begin your home-based business, put away the additional profit resulting from the reduced operational cost so you can afford to make the move out when you are ready.

You put the added margin into a future facility fund and fight off the tendency to use it. There is an important windfall for doing this. If you price your service or product based on its real value right from the beginning, you avoid losing your early buyers from sticker shock when you suddenly increase your prices to cover the new out-of-the-home overhead. This entire subject is about thinking as though you are running a full-blown business with all the costs including facility, insurance, phone and utility, internet, finance and accounting, other administrative costs, and overhead.

Another set of activities that solidifies the reality of an early home-operated business is corporate structure documentation. The documentation will vary depending on the type of business: S Corporation, LLC, Partnership, etc., and you will need your state and city operating licenses, incorporation papers, and to acquire your IRS, EIN, and DUNS numbers. Having these documents in place will lead to contracting a CPA to verify your accounting system and engaging an attorney to create the corporation. Some new business owners skip these incorporation steps and opt for just a company operating license, which may be sufficient. However, make sure you have a tax attorney evaluate the impact on your liability as a result of the business, which avoids you later wishing you had incorporated earlier.

It may be of interest to you to know how our CST location and facility environment evolved over time. Initially we launched the business in one room of an office building. This office building was designed to cater to start-up businesses like ours. When we won our first significant contract as a subcontractor our prime contractor offered space in their facility, so we moved into their offices. As we both grew over time and we began winning other contracts, we leased our own office space in the same facility.

As we continued to grow, we moved to a larger office complex and grew to a point where we were occupying an entire floor of the complex. At that point, our CFO researched the possibility of building our own building enabling us to apply the leasing costs to our own office facility which is what we did. Our CFO recommended we build a facility larger than we needed at the time allowing us to lease space to other companies, further financially supporting building our own facility. We stayed in our office building until we reached our liquidity event.

Following is a closing thought on location and your business success. This location guidance on planning and imaging not only applies to your location but to your ultimate business success. It goes beyond goal setting and planning; it requires employing imaging. The following pearl substantiates this:

> "Whatever the mind can conceive and believe,
> it can achieve."
> – NAPOLEON HILL

This pearl may seem trite at first but it's not. This concept has been written about and promoted for centuries and has become the centerpiece for successful human endeavors. Not understanding this and not developing this mindset is one of the most frequent shortfalls first-time entrepreneurs incur. The application of a combination of dreaming and imaging will lead to developing this persona and will spill over to your ultimate leadership team and can become the basis of your culture and could very well assure success and early profitability. It is basically putting real value on yourself. It has to do with understanding your own worth so you do not cheat yourself and, more importantly, your leadership team, or, ultimately, your family.

Initial Market Analysis and Business Development

I n the previous business plan discussion, we addressed market analysis and business development. These business topics are so vital to successfully launching a business that I want to expand on them here. In my experience, I've noticed that most people with a new business idea have rarely ever sold anything professionally. So, you may want to research the topics of market analysis and business development as you prepare to launch your business. I encourage you to do so since there are as many how-to-sell and market books and workshops as there are business ideas. In this section, I will share some market analysis and business development experiences that highlight some wise or not-so-wise decisions I've made relative to these topics.

In the early seventies following the successful Apollo Program lunar landing, a large number of us working on the program were disillusioned by the fact that most of the nation had lost its enthusiasm for space exploration and were preoccupied with the Vietnam War and President Nixon's resignation. I was among those disillusioned and disappointed people and was seeking a career change away from technology.

Since I was a weekend sailor and owned a twenty-six-foot competitive racing sailboat, I decided to move to a small town on one of the large Tennessee Valley Authority's lakes and start a sailboat marina. The marina idea fell through, so I started a boathouse and dock construction business as an alternative. My plan was to build a pile-driving rig and build strong and stable docks and boathouses around this lake by sinking creosoted pilings at least eight feet into the lake bottom as the foundation of my construction projects. As I got to know some of the new townspeople and was sharing my business plan with them, a large number of them were encouraging me to start this business because there was no apparent competition. Here's a pearl I wish I had thought of then:

> "If nobody else is doing it,
> it's probably a bad idea."
> – JAY NEWKIRK

As I contemplated launching this business, I talked to some of the local downtown business owners as well as some boat dock business owners about the idea. I, of course, got a lot of encouragement for doing it because they all knew there was a need. That market research was shortsighted. My conclusion that there was little or no competition was encouraging but unfortunate.

Months later, following a trying period of building and launching the pile-driving rig, I launched the business. To shorten a very interesting set of events and learning experiences, I came to the realization that there actually was real competition. There were a number of shade tree dock and boathouse builders that it seemed came from nowhere bidding against me on everything. I say "it seemed" because they had been there, but I missed identifying them in my market research. They were small mom-and-pop operations and not very visible.

In any case, their approach to boathouse and dock construction was to use fifty-five-gallon drum rickety platforms to hand drive bark-stripped cedar tree poles to shallow depths into the lake bottom and would build docks and boathouses on those rickety foundations for a lot less than I could. Of course, at the first freeze these poorly constructed boathouses and docks would just float away with the ice. Unfortunately, the customers could not see the fallacy in their construction vendor decisions which were being made during the warmer construction periods and were not taking into account the fallacy of building these structures on such weak foundations. They were erroneously choosing a cheaper option.

I struggled for a while and finally shut down the business. It was painful, but I learned a valuable lesson that prepared me later for more diligent market analysis. The point of the story is about competitive analysis. I was so determined to start the business that I could not see the weakness in my idea. So, as you contemplate and plan to launch a business, performing serious market and competitive analysis is critical. Based on the results of your analysis be prepared to adjust to those real results of deeper analysis. Another very important lesson here is that a no-competition environment can actually be a red flag that your business idea isn't a sound one.

Business Development Following the Initial Marketing

This discussion will focus on launching your business development activity following the initial market analysis. To begin with, what do I mean by *business development*? It is the activity of reaching out and contacting potential customers and selling them your services or products. In the government support services business, it starts with identifying what government agencies are physically close to your business location and ones you have identified in your initial market research that need what you have to offer. What you are doing in this early stage is creating a business development strategy and approach to selling your services and products.

During this early stage of launching CST, Bobby and I held some lengthy work sessions thinking through who we knew and who we had worked for or supported earlier in our careers. We both had been involved in supporting the government for a number of years, so we created our initial list of points of contact that we knew and who knew us, being careful not to approach any of them that would create a conflict with our current or past employers.

So, following that early market sector assessment we identified potential early buyers who sometimes were the customers who knew us and who we had supported and who had encouraged us to go into business. Some of them did become early customers. A very successful part of our early strategy was to continue to nurture these early customers. In addition to being early buyers we frequently encouraged them to provide us with referrals to other government people and organizations that they felt could use our services as well.

We have been discussing the strategy of early marketing and new business development in this section. After you have accomplished defining and refining this early strategy, you will need to move into the early stages of approaching these potential customers. There is an important lesson to be learned as you launch your selling activity. New and excited business owners and entrepreneurs struggle with trying too hard to sell. This normally comes from being excited about your new business and being excited about what you know how to do and on what you have based your business offerings. It's obvious that you should be excited about your offerings, but the approach should not be forcing or pushing what you know on your prospects. It's vastly more important that you focus on how what you know or what product you have can support what your potential customer *needs*.

Potential customers can sense your anxiety when you're pressing too hard, which results in what's been termed *buying it back*. So, this early business development approach is most successful when you climb inside the person's head you are approaching and visualize what they are thinking about you and your product or service. If you think they are viewing you as a professional with valuable offerings, then you will more likely be focusing on how what you have and what you do will support their achieving their objectives. This takes practice but mastering it will lead to surprisingly successful and rewarding results.

Developing Your Early "I Wants"

A significant element of my business consulting is that I consistently advise my clients to have clearly in mind their business outcome objectives. So, as you begin to launch your business and the business activity and operation initiates, you will need to take a moment to rethink *why* you have launched this business in the first place and what you want from it. It is important that you now recognize that you can affect early outcomes by developing a list of business "I Wants." The "I Wants" are business, not personal—they are what you want right now for the business. If you are comfortable with it, you should consider developing this list jointly with your closest associates. The business vision, mission, goals, and a glimpse of your personal dream will surface during the process. The pearl to keep in mind is:

> "People respond well to those
> that are sure of what they want."
> – ANNA WINTOUR

Examples of some "I Wants" at this early stage are:

- I want the company to be profitable from the beginning.
- I want to make sure the early employees and leadership team members have well-defined personal dreams.

- I want well-formed marketing flyers ready to support early business development.
- I want to create an early company culture and establish a positive work environment that results in a great place to work.

Your "I Wants" list will change and grow as the company begins to grow. You will need to continue revisiting, developing, and updating them as the company moves forward.

As we close this discussion on marketing, new business development, and our evolving "I Wants," I want to offer a reminder about the importance of keeping in mind overlaying everything we do with the three elements we discussed earlier: the human element, having a well-defined personal dream, and always applying outcome management. Having a succinct current list of business "I Wants" will support the evolution of optimized operating principles and processes and having them in place, right from the beginning.

PART THREE

Operating Principles and Business Processes

P art Three covers the company's overall operating principles and business processes with additional guidance for new business development (NBD), including best practices for RFP responses. From an operations perspective, we have to get our house in order before launching into an NBD year. That starts with knowing your plan for the year.

The meetings section follows, including techniques for launching the year with the annual kickoff meeting, which provides the leadership team (LT) input that assures the business plan includes the information needed to provide you and the LT the roadmap strategy needed for the coming year. The other operational meetings descriptions follow that initial information, which helps frame what the LT needs to be doing operationally on an ongoing basis for moving the company forward.

By having these operating principles and procedures in your mind in the early going—even before you may need them—you will be armed with having thought them through and you'll be ready when you need them in the future. That will lead to being prepared to successfully lead meetings when you have an expanded staff to lead.

Also, as a reminder, you should recall the discussion in Part One on the importance of overlaying the human element onto everything you do. Remember that running a business is an art requiring a delicate balance between tactical and strategic thinking. Here's the pearl on the subject:

> "Winners have the ability to step back from the canvas of their lives like an artist and gain perspective. They make their lives a work of art—an individual masterpiece."
> – DENIS WAITLEY

Waitley is referring to winners, which, in my opinion, include entrepreneurs, business owners, and leadership team members; so, he's speaking to you. Once the business has launched and you have held your annual kickoff meeting, it's time to focus on new business development, which is the operational activity that accomplishes the business plan's roadmap projections. Following the initial marketing analysis and the development of marketing material, the NBD activity is launched and starts with the process of opportunity identification and bid-no-bid decisions, followed by the proposal group's proposal factory kicking in.

The remainder of Part Three covers building a collaborative culture, including the leadership team's development with emphasis on their motivating the employees reporting to them through effective annual reviews.

I'll share an anecdote here on what we did during CST's early going. Before Bobby and I launched CST, I was working for Advanced Technology, Inc. (ATI) and was reporting to the president, Bob Larose. Since I had launched a successful ATI branch office in Huntsville, Bob and I had become close and he was supportive of my plans to launch my own company. When Bobby and I were developing our initial operating plan, we decided that I should travel to ATI's headquarters and meet with Bob and ask for his guidance and thoughts on optimizing our CST launch strategy. The outcome from that meeting and discussion was very informative and valuable, particularly since I shared with Bob that we were planning to follow ATI's strategy of growing CST to a significant revenue level over a ten-year period followed immediately by our liquidity event.

The reason I'm sharing this story with you is because, as I was talking with Bob, he reached over for a paper napkin and started making notes on it. The notes he made and subsequently gave to me include a lot of what I'm advising you to consider in this section on operating principles and business procedures. My meeting with him was a very important early milestone event and I want to do for you what Bob did for me—offer valuable guidance to help you succeed. My only regret is that I didn't frame that napkin and keep it.

Holding Successful Meetings

Over the years as I've conducted and attended meetings where there have been debates on the subject relative to the effectiveness of meetings and how many we really need to hold since they take time and, to some degree, detract from important operational activity. Here's a pearl as you think about how to hold meetings and how many to have:

> "Meetings should be like salt—a spice sprinkled
> carefully to enhance a dish.
> Too much salt destroys a dish. Too many meetings
> destroy morale and motivation."
> – JASON FRIED

It's clear that meetings are necessary, but they should be optimized, they need to be time constrained, and they should all have a well-thought-through agenda.

The subject of meetings has become almost controversial in the current fast-paced business environment. In my current consulting work, particularly with start-up companies led by young entrepreneurs, I have seen a movement away from many traditional business structure and processes including meetings. But meetings are still a necessary and important ongoing activity that need serious thought and preparation and are central to leadership teams moving forward collaboratively.

Meetings provide the necessary time and space to work through challenges. They ensure everyone is focused on the same ultimate company objective, and they continually serve to remind everyone why you're in business and that everyone is integral to the company achieving the agreed-to company objective.

Below I have included my guidance about how to conduct what I consider to be the most important types of meetings that you must hold in order to run and grow your business successfully.

A Note about Virtual Meetings

We had to make some important adjustments in the summer of 2020 because of the COVID-19 pandemic. There were work-at-home mandates ordered that led to holding virtual meetings using the internet and various video and conferencing platforms.

At first these meetings were awkward, but as the pandemic persisted virtual meetings were widespread and became more and more effective because the participants became comfortable with the virtual environments and these virtual applications improved. The live video images were positioned appropriately making room for shared meeting agendas, documents, and briefings. Also, chat-boxes became available so participants could text messages and questions as the meeting progressed. This also gave the facilitator the option to monitor the chat-box during the meeting and answer questions in real time or announce that following the completion of the agenda, items in the chat-box entries would be addressed.

So, what has become an effective outcome for the virtual meeting environment is that the number of meeting participants could be increased, and the participants could be located away from the meeting facilitator. Another positive outcome from this virtual meeting environment is that it may become the new-norm and ultimately become an ongoing meeting standard, which allows for a broader number of company employee participation and certainly saves on travel expenses. This meeting approach has led to succinct, time-activated, and clearly defined meeting outcomes. Over time another potential outcome is realizing that you may not need a particular meeting, which assures that the meetings you are now holding are effective.

Meetings have been changing in this environment, which is requiring you to succinctly prepare not only the agenda but also what outcome you want. Other important factors include the facilitator assigning someone to keep track of who's responsible for what and sending out a time-activated assignment worksheet to all participants and consider recording the meeting. Another pearl:

> "The majority of meetings should be discussions
> that lead to decisions."
> – PATRICK LENCIONI

Annual Leadership Team Kickoff Meeting

This is, by far, the most important meeting of all. Holding an annual kickoff meeting at or around the beginning of each year is imperative for business success. Stopping and taking time to review how your business did last year and comparing that against what's in store for the new year, provides an invaluable opportunity to ensure you know where you're going, strategically and tactically.

I know many business owners and leaders are busy with operational challenges. That should not stop you from holding this event to assess last year's performance and introduce what the new year holds. Doing so can set you up for success in the coming year and will help you stay on track with where you want to go.

There are basically three separate segments the meeting should cover:

1. **How Did We Do Last Year?**
   a. Did we reach last year's financial, head count, and bid-rate goals?
   b. If not, what are the reasons why?
   c. Operational highlights.

2. **Projections for the New Year**
   a. What are our financial goals for the new year?
   b. What other things are those goals based on, besides what we did last year?
   c. New year's operational plan.
   d. Do we have a preliminary pipeline developed?

3. **What Are We Doing as a Company and Why?**
   a. Do we have a clear idea of what it is our company actually does?
   b. Why are we doing what we do? Ask yourself:
      i. Are we doing something or offering a service simply because we know how, instead of because what we offer is relevant?
      ii. Are we doing it because we love it, or do we see a real need for our product and/or service and we really do want to help folks who need what we are offering?

There are loads of variations to the agenda for this meeting, and even more relative to the length of the event and its schedule. During the lunch break, you can consider inviting a keynote speaker to lead a motivational discussion, and you may need to include networking breaks during the event.

Following is an example agenda:

1. Opening Remarks – Pres/CEO
2. End of Previous Year Financial Review – CFO
   a. Discussion of Lessons Learned – Pres/CEO
3. Major Contract Reviews – COO/CFO
   a. Discussion of Lessons Learned – Pres/CEO
4. Operations Review and New Year's Plan – COO
   a. Discussion of Lessons Learned – Pres/CEO
5. New Business Dev. Approach and Pipeline – Bus Dev VP
   a. Discussion of Lessons Learned – Pres/CEO
6. Strategic Direction Plan – Corp Strategy VP
   a. Discussion – Pres/CEO
7. Financial Budget for New Year – CFO
   a. Discussion – Pres/CEO
8. Vision Discussion and Closing Remarks – Pres/CEO

After the event, be sure to summarize what went on and offer some of the outcome information to the participants and develop a message to all employees containing the company's new direction based on the outcome of this meeting. Sharing what was discussed with everyone will substantiate a collaborative culture and is motivating.

Mid-year Progress-to-date Meeting

This meeting is the sister meeting to the annual kickoff meeting. It is held in the middle of the company's fiscal year, usually mid-June. It is an extremely important meeting focused on providing a sanity check on how the company is doing relative to the annual company objectives and goals.

This meeting's agenda incorporates some of the items covered in the annual kickoff meeting including:

1. The CEO or the president introduces the COO, who summarizes the first half of the year's achievements.
2. Revisit the projections for the current year, including:
    a. Revenue
    b. Profitability
    c. Number of employees
    d. Number of contract wins
3. Lunch break with attendees networking

This meeting closes with the CEO or the president acknowledging and thanking the attendees for their contributions thus far while offering encouragement to meet the year-end objectives. Again, this is the opportunity to remind everyone what the company's ultimate revenue objective is and revisit why you're in business.

Weekly Leadership Staff Meetings

You, as the principal owner and company figurehead, have a responsibility to keep the company on course and weekly leadership staff meetings provide an important mechanism to achieving that. This meeting should be held Monday mornings in order to kick-off the week with action item assignments, identification of concerns needing attention, and a clear articulation of the desired outcomes for the week.

However, if you do not spend the time to prepare for these meetings, it can lead to your LT asking, "Why are we even having this meeting, anyway?" and they will be a waste of everyone's time and, worse, can lead to dampening the morale of your leadership team. And here again overlaying the human element strategy onto this weekly tactical business operational event can become central to the company's ongoing success.

So, before each of these meetings, sit back for a few minutes and reflect on how you achieved getting the company to its current state. Think on the mission and vision statements and reflect on your own personal dream. Doing this consistently brings clarity to how the company is doing at any given moment and leads to your conducting successful staff meetings. So, when you enter the staff meeting room, your leadership team will pick up on your focused and confident posture, and they will sense your genuine belief that the company is on its success path.

If you contemplate, at the moment you walk or log into these weekly staff meetings, how your team sees you, it becomes obvious and very important that you project to them what you believe they need to see. It will establish a feeling in the room or virtual environment that you know where you're going and will reiterate the need to "hold hands and run." So, you say it and remind everyone that you are serious about it.

Additionally, holding successful staff meetings begins with your overall attitude and how you treat people. As you become focused on successful growth and the word on the street is that your company is a great place to work and your team is working together collaboratively, your staff meetings are where this is reinforced. If you look at conducting your staff meetings effectively, they can turn in to secret weapons. How? Your competition will hear about your success and will scramble to acquire your pricing strategy or a copy of one of your proposals, or they will be trying to hire your leadership team members.

At CST, we locked down our LT by offering them stock options, cashable only at the liquidity event, and we also put in place annual leadership team performance bonus strategies. As a result, in the LT's community engagements and discussions they left positive impressions which impacted the competition, making it difficult for them to hire away our LT members. So, these forward-looking staff meetings had the outcome of locking down the LT, which is where my "secret weapon" thought came from relative to meetings.

In addition to my previous staff meeting advice, I want to share with you general meeting guidance from Larry Womack, author of the book *Outcome Management*, who states that, "A meeting should have an objective to inform, instruct, gather data, and/or celebrate and everyone should know the purpose of the meeting beforehand (agenda), its length, and its desired outcome." Following is some critical guidance from Larry that he shared in a blog on my website about how you should conduct every meeting:

1. Participants should receive the agenda beforehand.
2. The agenda should include a warm-up, a topic list with time-line, and the purpose of the topic—discussion, decisions, and/or other supportive information.
3. There must be a designated facilitator, timekeeper, and minute-taker.
4. Short of an emergency, there should be no interruptions.
5. There must be a next-action list and assignments.
6. There must be an evaluation of the quality of the meeting.
7. The minute-taker will provide all attendees copies of the minutes within two hours of the meeting's conclusion.

A practice we put in place as we were growing CST was to designate the third Monday morning staff meeting every month to a different agenda. This staff meeting was designed to have a quick review of how we were doing relative to our revenue, headcount, and profitability goals set at the annual kickoff meeting. The CFO would brief the leadership team on those metrics and if there were actions required we would have a brief discussion on them, make assignments, and move on to the primary objective of this important monthly meeting, which was to revisit why we were building this business together and where we were going.

At this meeting we reminded the attendees that the objective was to review what our annual company objectives were and then—most importantly—go around the room and ask members of the LT their thoughts on why we were building the business. We would ask a few members to share what they were going to do after we accomplished the corporate goal of reaching a revenue level of $100 million per year and achieving a successful liquidity event.

This consistent revisiting of why we were in business, our focus on the corporate ultimate objective, and frequently revisiting our individual personal dreams protected our culture of "holding hands and running," which is what set us apart from our competition—we knew where we were going, that we'd get there together, and we knew why!

Monthly Internal Support Staff Meetings

These meetings are basically operational meetings held and led by the Chief Technology Officer (CTO), Chief Financial Officer (CFO), VP Business & Administration, and the VP Business Development. The outcomes and action items resulting from these randomly scheduled internal support status meetings would normally be addressed by the leadership team members at the Monday morning staff meetings.

All-hands Meetings

These meetings are normally held quarterly and are designed to invite the entire staff to a luncheon meeting as a way to celebrate successes. The

CEO, president, or COO should address the staff with an overview of positive achievements to date, including articulating the company goals that were met since they were set at the annual kickoff meeting. This is another culture-protecting event where the employees realize that the leadership team appreciates their effort and contribution to the success of the company.

Another segment of this luncheon meeting is to recognize any staff members who have achieved outstanding work performance and also provides an opportunity to share overall staff announcements like new births, engagements, wedding plans, etc. A closing thought here is that this meeting can be held effectively virtually with all the agenda items intact with the exception of having lunch together.

New Employee Orientation Meetings

These meetings are held randomly based on the rate of new employees joining the company. The attendees of these meetings include the new employees and the leadership team and management staff. The objective of this meeting is to share with new employees the company policies and benefits and, most importantly, to introduce the new employees to the leadership team and management staff. At this meeting the CEO, president, or COO should share the company annual objectives and positive achievements to that point.

During our CST rapid growth periods, these meetings had the effect of substantiating our company's cultural goals of being focused on our employees achieving their personal career objectives working with us. Our HR director also created a very motivational environment during these meetings by connecting each new employee with one of the current leadership team members. Before the meeting began, the HR director wrote out famous quotes on slips of paper and cut them in half. As the new employees and leadership team entered the meeting, she handed the new employees one half of a quote and a leadership team member would get the other half. Everyone was told to find the person with the other half of their quote and to sit with them during the meeting and be prepared to introduce the other individual at the meeting's kickoff.

This activity taking place at a new employee orientation meeting was another event that substantiated that we, as company figureheads, were not all about ourselves but that our culture was about our employees. It also resulted in the new employees meeting the company leadership team. And it protected our collaborative company culture.

An interesting anecdote relative to one of these CST meetings was very gratifying. We had an employee at a particular meeting who had left CST for a job that offered him an increased salary, but he had returned to work at CST and was attending this employee orientation meeting. When it came time for him to introduce himself, he very succinctly addressed the other new employees and said, "I am a returning CST employee and want to make an important statement. I left CST for more money, but I quickly realized that it's not the money, it's the work environment. So, don't leave CST!" This employee was willing to come back to CST because we had created an inspiring environment to work in; you can imagine how gratifying that was to hear.

Project or Contract Status Meetings

These meetings are held at the operational level and are basically contract or project status meetings. Their frequencies vary based on the individual contracts' scopes of work requirements and they are held based on the project manager's preference and are very important for both the project managers and the employees. The structure of these meetings has evolved over time and emphasis has been placed on not drawing them out. Some PMs just have a daily fifteen-minute stand-up meeting quickly addressing each employees' current state, what's planned for the day, and what help they need from other project team members. This early morning meeting strategy has evolved from a new project management approach using a Scrum Strategy approach, which is an agile meeting framework that formalizes the stand-up meeting strategy mentioned above.

Meetings are obviously important and, in some cases, critical. It is up to you to create an ongoing set of meetings that work for you and your leadership philosophy. Just keep in mind that everything you do should be focused on helping others and that at every turn you are dealing with and interacting with people. Overlaying the human element strategy, as always, onto your meeting processes will ensure success and lead to effective outcomes.

New Business Development (NBD)

I discussed NBD in Part Two, but I want to expand on it here and emphasize that it is the most important element of successfully growing your company. However, emphasis on new business development must be balanced with sound operational performance and positive fiscal policy.

Clarifying What New Business Development Means

Below is a pearl and business development definition from a *Forbes* magazine contributor:

> "Business development is the creation of long-term value for an organization from customers, markets, and relationships."
> – SCOTT POLLACK

The conventional early guidance for launching a business is to develop a comprehensive business plan. Looking back at most business plan content, you will normally see a "Sales and Marketing" section but usually not one entitled "New Business Development."

First, you need to understand the difference between sales and marketing. Secondly, it's important to understand how and where new business development fits into the overall business activity. So, what is the difference between sales and marketing? Even though we discuss this business functional area as "sales and marketing," it should be reversed to "marketing and sales." That is because marketing is the earlier function, consisting of developing the strategy for sales as well as developing the marketing material and promotional activity that supports sales.

In the commercial retail and product business areas, "sales" is just that—selling the merchandise and/or the products. The other business focus is services. Services involves a broad range of activity including maintenance to support product sales, financial and accounting services, recruiting, and a host of other business support services.

In the governmental contracting support services area, there are, again, a wide range of activities including: software support, project management, Project Office support, information technology, cyber security assessment, etc. As a result of governmental programs and project growth, support services companies are being launched frequently and growing rapidly. After you and your company have successfully developed a marketing strategy and marketing material, including a vibrant company website and social media presence, your new business development team launches sales.

Sales and Marketing

In the early stages of growing a successful company, development of a well-thought-out sales and marketing approach is paramount to its early success. In this early growth stage of a business there may be some confusion about sales and marketing. These two operational activities are separate functions that need to be developed thoughtfully in the right order; marketing is first followed by sales.

The term *market research* captures the essence of what we mean by *marketing*. If you think about the term *research* relative to business growth, it means starting with asking yourself, Who are my potential clients? and What will I be offering them? Many start-up companies are launched based on having a past customer with a need for something you can produce, and the company has a built-in initial client. Soon after that, when the company has actually launched, the topic of new business development kicks in. If you then run out and try to sell something you will get hit with two questions you aren't prepared to answer creatively: "What does your company do?" and "Who are your current clients?"

Here is the important message about getting sales and marketing clearly thought through and in the right order. Before sales begins, you must have in-hand your initial marketing material. You must have thought through who your focused customer targets are and be prepared to clearly and succinctly articulate who they are. Otherwise the early sales visits will fail because the potential client will write you off immediately, concluding you don't have anything they need and, worse, you don't know where you're going. So, once you have created your initial marketing material and developed your marketing strategy, sales can begin successfully.

The New Business Development Practice

The elements of a successful new business development strategy start with knowing:

1. What is the branding strategy? What are you known for?
2. What are the core competencies?
3. What past performance experience do you have?
4. What are the capability strengths of the current staff?

5. What is the state of the market sector needs?
6. What are the business growth projections for the current year?

Launching or continuing a successful new business development strategy must include having clear answers to the above questions and, most importantly, having the leadership team members being in total agreement with the answers, which will result in achieving basic trust among the team members. The pearl is:

"A team is not a group of people who work together.
A team is a group of people who trust each other."
– SIMON SINEK

Marketing Preparation

Below is a list of important preparational marketing steps.

1. Prepare one-page capability statement flyers, rack-cards for conferences, and a capabilities summary briefing in preparation for business development meetings with potential clients and partners.
   a. Always carry with you your capabilities statement, a one-page flyer, or a glossy rack-card that captures who you are, professionally done and graphically designed with contact information.
   b. Be sure to include your DUNS Number, Cage Code, your designation (i.e. Service-Disabled, Veteran Owned, 8a, Woman Owned, etc.)
2. Identify and develop relationships with potential prime contractor partners. In preparation for visiting these potential

partners, it is very important to have identified a possible opportunity that you are tracking that you can bring to the meeting so you are offering something in addition to asking for a possible joint opportunity.

    a.   In developing your prime contractor relationships, identify large companies that are compatible with you for developing teaming relationships. Not necessarily companies that do what you do but find companies that need what you do. For example, perhaps an engineering firm isn't strong in IT, which you could bring to them to strengthen their bids.

3.   Identify potential government agencies and entities that have needs in your offering space. Plan to strategically visit with those requiring agencies' technical leads and their contracting officers.

4.   Identify and plan to attend conferences that potential clients are hosting, or ones focused on your offering areas.

5.   Join local professional organizations and attend their monthly meetings.

6.   Identify and attend local events focused on networking (chambers of commerce networking events, etc.)

At the beginning of a new business year and at your annual kick-off meeting, the leadership team member who is leading the business development activity should brief the other team members addressing these six elements. If they are not already clearly defined, then an important meeting outcome is for the leadership team to reach agreement on them. Remember this about sales:

> "Sales is not about selling anymore,
> but about building trust and educating."
> – SIVA DEVAKI

So, again, successful business development activity requires a balance between sales and marketing. There are sometimes differences of opinion among the leadership team members on the new business development focus and the priority of the activity. The issue, relative to this debate, centers on prioritizing the business development focus areas and, based on your size, deciding whether to pursue subcontracting opportunities versus priming.

Given a successful marketing activity outcome, the sales team takes that information and launches sales. Given that the marketing outcome is well organized and documented, the sales team develops a sales strategy and a priority list of potential clients and business development partners to visit. An important element of this sales planning is to perform an assessment of what conferences, seminars, and summits you plan to attend and develop a budget estimate for all the new business activities, trips, and associated expenses.

The 2020 COVID-19 pandemic environment has made a number of these events virtual, but attendance is still very important and many of the conferences are replicating the networking opportunities via video conferencing platforms. Even though these events are virtual we can still practice the human element in our NBD strategy!

Opportunity Identification

Right after successfully creating your sales and marketing strategy comes opportunity identification. This is another operational area that is frequently launched without enough strategic thought. First, opportunity identification varies greatly based on past performance, sphere of influence, communication skills, etc.

Initially it's about who you know and who knows your capabilities and strengths. Then comes identifying potential clients who need what you know how to do. Finally, it's about the people or companies who are already doing what you do. The latter group are your potential competitors so that is essentially competitive analysis.

Beyond those initial opportunity identification activities comes more formal approaches. As mentioned before, examples in the federal government contracting environment include attending potential client conferences; researching agencies' contract projections; joining professional organizations in your field of pursuit; and frequenting networking opportunities where competitors, partners, and potential clients are in attendance. You should also research companies who have systems and tools to support business development and opportunity identification. An example of one of these is Deltek Corporation's GovWin IQ offering. Once the strategy for identifying business opportunities has been developed and the opportunities are being identified, you must develop a tracking pipeline system to manage them.

Pipeline System Development

Most government support contractors develop a pipeline spreadsheet that prioritizes the identified opportunities. A spreadsheet should be designed which includes:

- the opportunity's contract name
- the government contract tracking number
- the agency contracting offices' points of contact
- the request for proposal (RFP) release date
- the RFP proposal due date

This pipeline design allows for searching the spreadsheet for the contracting agencies and the contract release and proposal due dates in order to find what agencies are in the pipeline data and to identify what opportunities have close-in dates for which preparation is needed.

There are several commercial and government websites that can be searched and monitored for the purpose of identifying opportunities that support building the pipeline spreadsheet, including:

1. DelTek GovWin Government Opportunities Searches https://www.deltek.com/en/products/business-development/govwin

2. The new consolidated GSA MAS Site for Specific Special Item Numbers (SINs) https://gsa.federalschedules.com/resources/gsa-mas-consolidation/#phase-one

3. Government agencies' Opportunity Forecasts Example is NASA's MSFC Forecasts can be found at: https://www.hq.nasa.gov/office/procurement/forecast/ and click on MSFC.

4. DOD Office of Small Business Forecasts see: https://business.defense.gov/Small-Business/Acquisition-Forecasts/

5. The former FedBizOps site, now beta.SAM.gov see: https://fbohome.sam.gov/

In addition to the above ongoing activity, the company's business development lead briefs the leadership team weekly or biweekly at recurring business development status meetings. This new business development status briefing could be included in the weekly staff meeting and includes sharing the business development opportunity pipeline, identifying the close-in opportunities of interest, and closes with the status of any ongoing proposal activity.

Your company's new business development processes and approaches are unique to your company. So, it is very important that the business development lead put in writing the strategy and approach and be prepared to brief the leadership team on the status of the activity so everyone concurs with the new business and pipeline development approach. This is critical since everyone in a growing company sells.

Priming vs. Subcontracting

This discussion topic addresses the decisions associated with responding to an opportunity as the lead participant—the prime—in a partnering response versus being a teammate in a partnering response where you will be a subcontractor to a partner who will lead the response and, if it is won, will lead the execution of the contract.

When you are preparing to respond to an opportunity in a partnering situation, the decision associated with priming versus subcontracting is, to a large degree, subjective. There are several factors to consider if you plan to prime an effort including:

1. Has your company held a prime or subcontract for this client earlier?
2. Has your accounting system been audited?
3. Do you have the financial strength to manage the contract and a sufficient bank line of credit?
4. Are you technically capable of executing every line item in the performance work statement?
5. Are your internal support staff, the facility space, and infrastructure sufficient to execute the contract successfully?

Another prime versus subcontracting decision consideration has to do with an overall growth strategy. As a new or start-up company there is real evidence to support subcontracting versus priming in the early going. As a subcontractor you can focus on technical contract performance and your deliverables while the prime deals with all the contractual and administrative issues allowing you to gain experience and past performance history as you prepare to become a prime contractor.

Once the approach is considered and the business development strategy is agreed upon, the work begins. This includes opportunity identification and establishing the sources for finding them and developing a strategic process for execution.

Bid-no-Bid Decisions

Having identified an opportunity whose scope of work fits your offerings, you then must make a well-thought-through bid-no-bid decision. In other words, you have to ask yourself two questions:

1. Do we have the technical and financial strength to bid this effort?
2. Can or should we prime the effort, or should we identify a potential prime contractor partner?

Another important decision factor relative to bidding or not bidding on a given contract opportunity has to do with what time and effort has been put into introducing yourself and your company to both the potential client and possible partnering companies. The win probability is directly proportional to the success of this preliminary activity.

A proposal submitted to a potential client who doesn't know you or expecting a prime contractor who doesn't know you to take you on as a subcontractor has a very low probability of being considered or ultimately winning the contract. The preparation for bidding on a contract is as important if not more important than submitting the proposal response itself. The associated pearl is:

> "If I had eight hours to chop down a tree,
> I'd spend six hours sharpening my axe."
> – ABRAHAM LINCOLN

In my personal experience in the high-tech federal government contracting environment in Huntsville, Alabama, start-ups and young companies have consistently subcontracted early on. In fact, one company developed a strong and ongoing relationship with a successful prime contractor and exclusively subcontracted with them for several years. It wasn't until they had reached 300 employees and millions of dollars in annual revenues before they broke into becoming a prime contractor themselves.

So, for a new company or an ongoing one, new business pursuit requires comprehensive and simultaneous development of well-planned sales and marketing strategies, a well-organized opportunity identification process, a comprehensive pipeline tracking system, understanding of the pros and cons of priming versus subcontracting, and developing a focused bid-no-bid decision process.

The Proposal Factory

A s you are refining your business processes working toward sustainment and securing longevity you will need to achieve proposal excellence, which leads to building company value. You and your company are now defining and refining your business processes and may have already been in the business of writing some proposals and winning contracts. You are about to take the company to the next level and start building value as viewed from the outside. To sustain the necessary growth efficiently and consistently, you will need to refine your opportunity discrimination approach and streamline your proposal process.

When you start to seriously consider streamlining your proposal process and developing a replicable opportunity selection strategy and ultimately adopt a well-oiled proposal process, it is important to be able to translate the essence of this chapter's message and guidance by adapting it for your industry, your target client base, your offerings, and the development stage of your company.

In terms of proposing for work, the principles covered here will apply whether the request for proposal response is an informal short few pages; a forty-five-day, 100-page formal government proposal; a seven-day, ten-page task-order response; or a sophisticated commercial RFP response submittal. The point is, you must structure a process that is replicable so you do not have to start from scratch every time you decide to submit a bid.

The beginning point for constructing a proposal factory is assessing, critically, what you have in your past proposal repository. By "critically" I mean open-mindedly reviewing what reference files you have gathered and submitted so far, finding all filed past proposal material, and reviewing separately the management volumes, the past performance write-ups, staffing plans, cost volume sections, and any contract transition plans you've proposed. The key is to develop a pipeline, structure a bid opportunity selection process, write responsive proposals, win contracts, and build backlog.

Responding to RFPs to win contracts with the federal government is an ongoing effort for businesses and entrepreneurs involved with federal contracting. And keeping pace with the ever-changing and dynamic environment poses unique challenges that entrepreneurs need to be ready for so they can respond quickly and win.

Frequently, small businesses are juggling so many tasks, including day-to-day operational decisions and recruiting and hiring, that developing a solid proposal response system falls by the wayside. Coupled with not having clearly identified the target market sector, small businesses can struggle to successfully win these contracts.

Following is some basic information on the successful proposal process, including the proposal team members and their roles. Included will be some guidance on how to overlay the human element into this process, which can optimize successful contract proposal submittals. The proposal team members and their responsibilities are shown below.

1. **Capture Manager**: together with their team, is accountable for business development methodologies and, once an opportunity is identified, to capture information needed to support development of a winning proposal.
2. **Proposal Manager**: coordinates the proposal plan and coordinates proposal contributors including the production management staff.

3. **Proposal Coordinator:** administers proposal processes by ensuring high-quality configuration management.

4. **Subject Matter Experts:** improve the quality of a proposal by providing specialized expertise and proposal input.

5. **Technical Writers:** write the content and define illustrations to be used in the proposal.

6. **Review Team:** members of this team are assigned different sections of the proposal to review at designated times.

7. **Graphic Artists:** design proposal illustrations and integrate them into the final proposal.

8. **Desktop Publishers:** ensure that formats and typographic styles are compliant with the RFP instructions.

After a proposal opportunity has been identified and a bid decision is made, the capture manager hands off the leadership of the proposal development to the proposal manager. He or she then assembles the proposal team and, with the help of the proposal coordinator, develops a detailed schedule that clearly identifies important milestones key to completing the proposal in time to meet the submittal date requirement.

Keep in mind that this guidance assumes that your company is at a growth stage where individuals can be assigned these various roles. In the early stages, it's likely that you and a few others will take on all these roles. However, it's important that these roles be executed as you grow into the ability to distribute the responsibility.

The Human Element Strategy and the Proposal Process

The human element strategy we've discussed earlier is a strategic element in the proposal process and in developing the proposal factory. It's important to address the critical step of motivating the proposal team at the outset. By doing so, you can ensure that everyone has a helping-one-another mindset and that the RFP response will be created with the right readers in mind. Remember, you must get inside the head of the proposal evaluators and be sure that you meet their expectations. This starts with the company leadership supporting the capture and proposal managers and the coordinator, helping them address the following questions:

1. Who is this potential client?
2. What do they do?
3. What is their mission and vision?
4. What are the client's "hot buttons"?
5. What challenges are they facing that caused them to release the RFP in the first place?

This process leads into defining a set of one-liner themes that will get woven into every volume of the proposal.

The Proposal Response Process

Prior to holding the proposal kickoff meeting, the company leadership meets with the capture manager and proposal manager. During this meeting, the capture manager shares everything they've learned about the potential customer. The capture manager further shares that there will be a customer proposal evaluation team and it will be important to identify and profile the evaluation team and its leadership, which provides the proposal writers insight so their response can hit the prospective client's expectations throughout the responses' write-ups. At the kickoff meeting, the proposal manager shares all the information they have learned. Then the group agrees on the theme statements that the writers will ultimately internalize, leading them to work those themes into the writing where possible.

One of the success keys to this proposal team meeting is for the group to study the RFP proposal instruction section and internalize what is critical to the evaluation criteria section. This leads to refining the theme development activity. It is important in the development of proposal themes that they be captured and structured so they can literally be copied into the text. Additionally, they should not be so long that they can't be easily internalized by the proposal technical writers. Keep them as simple and pointed as possible.

An Example

Let's say the client is a government program office responsible for upgrading an important weapon system that has aged and is not serving our men and women in uniform well when they're counting on it to successfully support their defense of our nation in critical engagements. A typical US Army weapon system program office is almost always led by a uniformed officer—a Bird Colonel and possibly a full General Officer.

These are the potential client types who are passionate about their troops and making sure the weapon system's program office is providing them with what they need to complete a critical mission successfully. So, following is some guidance and some example text for your theme statements, applicable to this example:

1. "Our company's weapons development approach has been assuring your troops are equipped with leading-edge tactical systems that protect them and assure success. Our track record for doing that well will be key to our upgrade plan for your [system name]."

2. Then give an example of a similar successful system upgrade your business performed in an earlier contract. These are important substantiation statements that get scored high by the proposal evaluators.

3. Other shorter theme statements can include: "Our troop-friendly systems assure . . ." and "In systems upgrade projects similar to yours we have successfully . . ."

When we reached this business process refinement point at CST, we were ready to move the company to the next level and were ready to bid on what we then termed *wide-body* opportunities. At this point in CST's growth activity, the US Federal Government's General Services Administration (GSA) released a large indefinite delivery, indefinite quantity (IDIQ) RFP. It was designed to be awarded up to ten winners, so it was termed a *multiple-award contract*. It was a bold step for a company our size—approximately 200 employees—to pursue, particularly since it was being released as a "full and open" competition, meaning that there were no restrictions on the size of the companies who could bid on it. We would be going up against some well-established large companies with large bid and proposal budgets. We spent serious time assessing our approach and probability of winning it, then made the decision to bid, got focused on it, and did, in fact, write a killer proposal. We were selected as one of the ten winners.

As one of the winners, we earned the right to bid on the IDIQ contract's ongoing task order releases that would come out under the basic contract. Here is the bottom line of this story and how it applies to the topic of proposal factories. When the client released a task order for the ten winning companies to bid on, we had seven days to respond to the task orders' request for proposal with a serious page limitation, sometimes as few as ten pages and up to about thirty. The realization of what we were going to be up against turned the company around. We knew that we had to streamline our proposal response process and get ready for these potential releases. So, our CST proposal factory was born.

Our proposal leadership team member took on the task of creating the process, assembling the database of our entire past proposal material, organizing it into accessible files, and then outlined how we could optimize its application to task order responses. So, from then on we responded to every task order that came out of the IDIQ contract and, in doing so, our proposal team refined the response process and could turn out what looked like a forty-five-day proposal product in seven days. We won almost all the task orders released by the contract during the first two years of the contract, which doubled the size of our company and the revenue base. Here's a pearl to help you as you navigate creating your proposal factory:

> "I don't care how much power, brilliance or energy you have; if you don't harness it and focus it on a specific target, and hold it there, you're never going to accomplish as much as your ability warrants."
> – ZIG ZIGLAR

Another important detail you need to include in creating your proposal factory is streamlining retrieving past proposal material and adapting it for use in a current response and making sure you update the graphics to assure the look is new and fits the current potential client's expectations. Since those early days of IDIQ contracting and CST's development of what was then a state-of-the-art proposal response system, several proposal product companies have developed well-documented systems for achieving this result.

So, it does not matter what system you adopt for capturing the past data and information you need for ongoing proposal responses. If you and your team have not bought into refining that capturing process, adopting it, and collectively using it consistently to respond to fast turnaround proposal requirements, you will not accomplish the desired outcome. Whatever system you adopt is just a tool. It is your team's using it effectively and being committed to each other that leads to winning proposals. Adopting the process, optimizing its use on every response, and always staying focused on the current requiring entity's desired outcome will lead to your proposal success. So, the factory and the process are tools; it is the team's focus and attitude that are key.

So, are proposal factories important? Based on you and your leadership team's growth objectives, absolutely. The processes and accessibility of all past proposal material and the ability to edit it efficiently to fit any given customer's requirements led to CST's successful outcome. The applicable pearl here is:

> "It's not the will to win that matters, everyone has that. It's the will to prepare to win that matters."
> – PAUL "BEAR" BRYANT

Applying the Psychology of Winning to the Proposal Process

Using the proposal factory and its processes comes with a price. Pressure, stress, and anxiety build during intense proposal periods and can lead to the leadership team losing basic people sensitivity and forgetting that the company's underlying theme is about helping each other and holding hands and running. Dream-building and focus on reaching the company's ultimate exit strategy need to be ongoing topics of discussion at strategy meetings and breaks during these proposal engagements. Constant communication and use of spot bonuses following wins becomes very important. The pearl is:

> "It is not in the pursuit of happiness that we find fulfillment, it is in the happiness of pursuit."
> – DENIS WAITLEY

This applies not only to your company's staff and proposal team members, but also to the potential client to whom you are proposing. Here lies another one of the subtleties of success. We have discussed earlier that you, your leadership team, and your company will prosper if you can constantly keep in mind how the people you are dealing with, to include people you are proposing to, view you. Remember, you must get inside the other person's head and look back at yourself and be responsive to what you perceive they see. When you do that, you will begin to respond differently and more effectively to people in front of you as well as to the proposal evaluators who your proposals are targeting. You will begin to share in your responses what the client needs, and they will realize that you have the ability to solve *their* problem. It will change your delivery and your focus, will eliminate writing "tutorial" proposals, and you will find yourself delivering exactly what the potential customer is looking for.

This seems very straightforward, but it is not. Because of our natural human and survival instincts, we tend to push onto others what we are thinking, and we are constantly selling our ideas at work, at home, and all around. It takes real concentration and a strong intention to climb into someone else's head, look back at yourself, and say to them what they need and want to hear. Again, it is an art, and you must practice it in your proposal responses in order to optimize your win rate.

In the proposal environment, practicing this strategy is about spending serious time with the writing contributors, sharing with them what this customer is looking for, and imploring them to visualize the evaluators sitting alone reading your material hoping that you know and care about what *they need*. The reason this is such a challenge is that people who have started a company and are passionate about their product or service tend to push what they know and what offerings they have rather than think in terms of how they can adapt what they know and have to solve a potential client's particular requirement.

As we move on in this discussion, the assumption is that you are working toward achieving sustainment and growth and anticipating moving your company to a position of optimal value. When we were at this juncture at CST, the operational structure was evolving, and several operational divisions were formed around pursuing work with a number of the existing government agencies. Another consideration at this point in our company's growth was to organize around several of our technology focus areas. Since we were refining our proposal factory, the decision was made to organize around the government agencies we were targeting in order to avoid our operating divisions competing for opportunities on the basis of technology rather than agencies. So, we organized our proposal factory to respond to agency solicitations and pulled our past performance and other proposal inventory as needed and adapted it as required for the relevant agency requirements.

As we continued to grow, we learned that the psychology of winning applied to the proposal process was no different than applying it to success in general. Denis Waitley, in his book entitled *The Psychology of Winning* published in 1986, addresses it in terms of human honesty and aligning thought, word, and action. He also addresses success by assuring that you are focused on goals and not being distracted by time-wasting activities. Here's one of his quotes and another pearl to help you stay focused:

> "Don't confuse activity with accomplishment."
> – DENIS WAITLEY

The study of the psychology of winning deals with an individual's achieving: self-expectancy, self-image, self-control, self-esteem, self-awareness, self-motivation, self-direction, self-discipline, self-dimension, and self-projection. Below is a translation of some of these personal attributes to your company.

Self-image

It is my opinion that you or your company cannot achieve success without reaching a very positive self-image point. There has been a lot written about how to achieve this as an individual and few people have been able to understand how to achieve it. It starts with letting go of any mental baggage being carried from a person's early life that reinforces thoughts about "I can't," "I won't," or "I don't deserve," that have been carried into their adulthood. Individuals must give themselves permission to achieve their dreams, and image and focus on them daily. As the founder and leader of your organization, you have to exude this mentality, or your leadership team will not stay with you. People will follow someone who knows where they're going.

Once you have achieved buy-in from your leadership team, it is time to call them together and create a "company self-image." How? The first step is to create the equivalent of a personal dream for the company in the form of the ultimate corporate liquidity objective. We have discussed earlier the importance of making sure your leadership team members each have a personal dream they are moving toward by working with you and your company. In order to achieve the equivalent "company dream," the proposal factory must be formed and operating optimally. In addition, the proposal team and the leadership team must come together and lock on to where the company is going and assure that the proposal responses and work being pursued are moving the company toward its ultimate objective.

Assuming the leadership team collectively believes the company objective is achievable and they continually profess it, the company will be viewed as a great place to work and viewed by the employees, the customers, and even the competition as knowing where it is going and will have achieved a positive company self-image.

Self-control

This attribute for an individual is achieved through several important influences, including family, spiritual foundations, and individuals in their sphere of influence. In the case of the company, self-control is established primarily by the founders and key leadership team members including the comptroller and CPA. This leads to a very important element of the proposal factory. The proposal process must contain a disciplined opportunity discrimination component that provides a self-control mechanism to evaluate and discriminate from all the potential opportunities entering the pipeline.

In the case of individual self-control, it's an expression of maturity. Once you have brought your company to a point of solid sustainment and growth, you will have reached an important level of corporate maturity which will be manifested in a successfully operating proposal factory. The process you have put in place will be working as the entire leadership team and the proposal professionals will have realized that the opportunity discrimination function is working and that everyone understands what blue birds are and unanimously reject them. An important pearl to remember is:

> "Remember, you always have a choice. If you don't want to do something, or if it doesn't take you closer to your goal, it's OK to say no."
> – MELITTA CAMPBELL

Self-esteem, Self-awareness, Self-motivation

Esteem, awareness, and motivation can be integrated when viewed or framed relative to a corporation. In an earlier chapter we discussed applying the critically important pearl that, "It's not about me, it's about you."

Another vital pearl discussed was, "I'm not who I think I am, I'm not who you think I am, I'm who I think you think I am." Remember this second one is about getting inside the head of the person you are dealing with at the moment and understanding how they perceive you and then responding accordingly. As an individual, you cannot conduct yourself in that manner without a certain amount of self-esteem, self-awareness, and self-motivation. Let's translate this into the corporate environment.

Image one of your competitors, a potential employee, or a customer accessing your corporate website. They hit the site and up pops your home page. If you think about that for just a second you realize that your company's self-esteem, self-awareness, and self-motivation make an initial impression when the website opens. This is where the following pearl we introduced earlier is again applicable:

> "You only have one chance to make a good first impression!"
> – DAN PEÑA

Another example of establishing these corporate attributes is through encouraging your leadership team and key employees to attend self-improvement and motivational training seminars. The corporate posture and profile as viewed from the outside are framed by the image of the company as projected by these individuals daily. The final and most important activity that will assure positive corporate self-esteem, self-awareness, and self-motivation is that one staff meeting per month be devoted to the equivalent of a dream session, except in this case it is focused on whether the company is staying on track relative to the proposal process resulting in successful pursuits and contract wins that are moving you toward the company's ultimate liquidity value.

A Final Word

Working toward and ultimately establishing a proposal factory becomes a key factor in achieving your company's success. In doing so, the leadership team and key employees along with a majority of the entire workforce can sense that the company is successful and moving toward important milestones. The community surrounding the company is beginning to see that you and your company are emerging as an important contributor to the area's economic growth and that you and your team are beginning to give back by supporting and contributing to your chamber of commerce and the community's charitable activity. Your proposal factory lays the groundwork to keep you motivated, focused, and sustained.

Recruiting and Hiring

I f you're just starting out and don't even have employees or a leadership team yet, you nevertheless still need to be thinking about your recruiting and hiring strategy and approach.

It's important in these early stages to develop operating principles and procedures that you can refer to when you need them later, instead of trying to develop them when you wish you had them. How you approach hiring will lay the foundation for ensuring that you bring people into your business who share your dream and vision for the company. It is not enough to simply hire someone who can fulfill the role—if you want your company to ultimately succeed you must hire people for their outlook and positive attitude, not just their resume content. Your hiring strategy and your resulting workforce contribute to your overall corporate culture, which can make or break your business.

If you have motivated and positive employees who love to come to work and are eager to help fulfill the company's ultimate objective, you will have a corporate mentality that leads to stability, profitability, and positivity. You will develop a culture of people helping other people. If, however, your workforce is unmotivated, negative, and questions their value to you and the company, this will be reflected not only in their work but also in their attitudes. And guess who will experience firsthand this negative attitude? Your customers.

Your employees are the gateway to your customers. If your employees are excited about working for you and the company, your customers will know. If they're not, your customers will inevitably know that, too, which could ultimately lead to your company's failure. Adapting an appropriate, people-focused hiring process early on protects you from having to deal with a negative, unmotivated workforce down the road. Whether you have a product or services business, your employees are your greatest asset and will ultimately determine your success.

Applying the Pearl

Zig Ziglar is credited with saying, "You will get all you want in life if you help enough other people get what they want." I modify this pearl slightly, below, to help you apply it to your hiring process (my addition is in italics):

> "You will get all you want in life if you help enough other people *with a dream* get what they want."

The addition of "with a dream" is critical to the hiring process—and business success in general. When interviewing employee candidates you have a choice about your approach. You can start by interrogating them about their work history and past performance (which you should already know, otherwise you shouldn't have brought them in for an interview) and administer detailed and sometimes intimidating tests. Or, you can overlay your hiring process with the human element strategy to bring in the best possible candidates.

You should know the candidate's ability to do the job prior to their even coming in for an interview because you've already done a pre-interview analysis and assessment by calling references, talking with current employees with knowledge of the candidate, and searching for legitimate insight on the candidate's makeup and past performance. Researching the applicant will lead to an interview environment that is about determining if the job is right for the candidate.

The following is an example situation: A candidate is in your office, excited about joining your company and making a career move. The interview begins and the candidate starts expounding on his or her ability to perform in this position. You stop the interview suddenly, not rudely, and say, "I appreciate your wanting to sell yourself and convince me that you can do this job well, but you would not be here if I did not already believe you could do the job. Instead, we need to spend this time together determining if this job is *right for you* and if working here will move you toward your personal dream." Then you ask the candidate, "What is your dream?" It's important here to let the silence work for you, so sit quietly and observe the candidate's reaction to the question.

To the traditional HR professional this question and approach may seem absurd. It is not. It's actually the key to the ultimate success of your company. By asking every candidate this question you are looking beyond the candidate's ability to perform on your job opening position, you are looking past even their career goals; you are looking for them to open up to you and tell you what they would do if their work with your company resulted in their achieving significant success and they found themselves with sufficient resources to do almost anything they wanted to do. You can also ask this question specifically: "What would you do if you were financially free?"

Now, I don't want this interview strategy to be misleading. I know that traditionally you must have a dialog with a candidate and for technical positions you must make sure the candidate can perform the work. What this approach I'm sharing with you is about, particularly for interviewing senior program managers and leadership team members, is, again, overlaying the human element on every engagement. This is an example of that in your interview process.

Some interviewees will be right on top of answering this question. Others will struggle with it because they haven't ever thought about it. As you observe the candidate's response to the question, you are looking for a positive continuing dialog that leads to you helping them start thinking about it. However, if the candidate gives you the feeling that they think your question is irrelevant and they're not really interested in answering it or you detect a negative attitude about it, this may not be the candidate you're looking for. The outcome of this kind of interview process results in a leadership team and employees who know you care about them and that you have agreed, right from the start, that the job fits their future view and everyone's expectations are on the table at the outset.

We applied this approach consistently throughout CST's fourteen-year history. As the leadership team grew, the culture formed around the common understanding that we were focused on helping each other reach our dreams. This approach to interviewing and building a cohesive team is not an exact science, but if you are sincere and apply it consistently, a majority of the team will trust one another, will collaborate, and the desired culture will be established and maintained. Remember, to paraphrase Dexter Yager, "You can run with a hundred easier than you can drag one."

Another important outcome from applying this hiring approach is that it will immediately become obvious if some people without a dream or with negative attitudes slip through. They will usually try to change the culture to their way of thinking. However, if you hold fast to your positive environment philosophy, they will very likely purge themselves because they can't stand the positive environment. If they don't, then you must remove them. Doing so quickly and professionally substantiates to the remaining team that you are willing to do whatever it takes to protect the team and the culture, and that you really are about helping other people get what they want.

Remember, your employees are an extension of you and represent your company at every turn. You must believe in them and trust them. If you do, they will know it, and everyone will work together to help each other achieve their individual and professional objectives and dreams.

Leadership Team Growth with Culture in Mind

Leadership team growth is accomplished in two ways: growing and maturing your existing leaders and recruiting leadership team members carefully. So, while maturing your existing team members, be sure to focus on being particularly cautious about bringing in new leadership team members. You are looking for candidates with a dream and who have clearly defined career objectives. As discussed earlier, you want to be sure that their position in your company is going to move them toward their personal objectives and, ultimately, to their dream. Focusing on this during the recruitment and hiring process will be essential to assuring success as you grow your company.

Leadership team growth starts with understanding and developing a culture based on an "open-door policy." This is a concept that is not very well understood and there has been little specific guidance on how to develop it and how to protect it.

The CST practice of an open-door policy was based on our leadership team members being comfortable meeting with and having ongoing discussions and dialog with employees at every level in the organization. The culture developed around the idea that we were about helping each other. So, when we had challenges and/or were developing new technology and the leadership team had strategic and operational input, we got into discussions about it at any and every level. This essentially defined our culture. Like any organization, we had a hierarchical structure but, operationally, we had a flat organization with open dialog among different operating groups and at every level. We worked at not competing with ourselves.

Since I've been working for a number of years, I can recall earlier management environments that tolerated managers who competed with one another resulting in a "closed door" cultural environment. Therefore, you will have to be diligent in assuring that no one with that mindset works their way into your company. Ensuring that your leadership team understands and has internalized this open and collaborative environment concept automatically protects your culture.

Continuing to emphasize this concept is basic to creating a positive work atmosphere which is based on trust and a collaborative work environment. If you practice it and protect it and have developed that culture and a positive work environment and have a leadership team that holds hands and runs together, no one can stop you.

You will flourish under this kind of collaborative work environment, but you have to be serious and strong about it because you will be attacked internally and externally by the 80 percenters of the population whose outlook is skeptical and blame-based. Here is where, again, I make the important point that building a successful business takes inner strength and perseverance. I want to emphasize that if you are willing and able to overcome your pre-business sphere of influence—those people who will be wanting to, like crabs in a basket, drag you back—you will win. You will have to be vigilant and focused and have your own dream intact because it is your dream that will pull you through.

Again, it's important to protect the work environment and your positive culture, so be particularly cautious when bringing new members into the leadership team. Always check for the presence of a dream and assure that their position in your company is going to lead them to accomplishing their career goals and their dream. This very important practice will anchor the company and assure success during every phase of its growth.

Focusing on protecting your culture through leadership development and executing it well will result in your desired outcome.

By way of closing this section on "Leadership Team Development with Culture in Mind," let me summarize the subject matter one more time. Your leadership development includes recruiting successfully. So, you are protecting the culture by recruiting and hiring people who understand your emphasis on culture. During your recruiting and hiring activity, protecting the culture must be on your mind. A recruitment failure point results from interviewers sometimes only focusing during their discussion on what a candidate knows so they are examining the applicant during the entire interview process which puts the candidate on the defensive so that, if hired, they never forget their first impression.

Successful leadership team recruitment and overall growth in numbers, including the individual team member's personal growth, has to do with developing a positive and collaborative culture and continually reinforcing it with an open-door policy and discussing it in meetings and at events so it's consistently clear to everyone.

Putting this into practice and emphasizing it operationally while teaching your leadership team to recruit and hire successfully will ultimately create a company that one day will win the "Best Place to Work" annual award.

The Annual Review Process

In this section we've discussed practices and operational approaches that contribute to shaping the company culture. The heart of it is overlaying decisions and communication with the human element. No place is this practice more valuable than when we are dealing with our employees, who are our company's greatest assets. Here's a pearl to substantiate this:

> "If you honor and serve the people who work for you,
> they will honor and serve you."
> −MARY KAY ASH

This is a priceless pearl that, when applied to your engagements with your employees, will create a workforce that is sincere, committed, and excited about where you're taking the company.

We have discussed the human element strategy in the recruiting and interviewing process. If handled well with a candidate while discussing your focus on your employees' individual success and growth, they will never forget it. This leads to another important operational activity, the annual review process and overlaying it with the human element strategy. The steps that make up this review process include:

1. Hold a supervisors' meeting to provide annual review and pay raise guidance
2. Distribute employee Self-assessment Form
3. Employee returns Self-assessment Form
4. Supervisors conduct review with employee and completes Performance Review Forms
5. Employee Review Forms delivered to HR for processing
6. Inform employees when pay raises go into effect

The content of the Employee Self-assessment Forms initiates the human element impact of the pending review. The employee gains insight into what is important to the company relative to employee performance. Typical assessment form questions for the past year's performance include:

1. Description of Current Job Duties
2. Achievements and Successes
3. Weaknesses and Failures
4. Collaborative Efforts
5. Collegiality with Coworkers
6. Supervisor Feedback
7. Performance Goals
8. Wishes for Professional Development
9. Long-term Goals Within the Company
10. Additional Information

In addition to these standard questions, an additional human element question is: What type of work would you like the company to pursue? The employee's answer to this question moves the review into sharing the company's growth strategy and culture development based on employees reaching their career goals, which again accomplishes the company achieving its ultimate corporate goals and objectives.

PART FOUR

Stabilize and Anchor

You launched the business and it's growing. We've covered operating principles and business processes so now it's time to stabilize and anchor your company and drive it deep before you go wide. You should review why you're building this business anyway. It's a dream and it's yours. Remember:

> "Every great dream begins with a dreamer. Always remember, you have within you the strength, the patience, and the passion to reach for the stars to change the world."
> – HARRIET TUBMAN

Let us start this discussion with clarifying what *stabilizing* and *anchoring* your business means. In Part One I discussed founding principles including applying the human element at every busines engagement. I discussed the importance of having a dream and the importance of practicing outcome management at every turn. In Part Two I discussed successfully launching the business and in Part Three I introduced the basic operating principles and business processes important for early successful growth.

115

So, stabilizing the company is accomplished by assuring that the leadership team and all project managers understand the above principles and processes and are continually practicing them. Anchoring the company is accomplished by focusing on those principles and processes, identifying contractual opportunities, positioning your company to bid on them, responding to their proposal scopes successfully, and, ultimately, winning a majority of them.

Internalizing those principles and applying those processes leads to stabilizing and anchoring the business, which is accomplished by applying all of that guidance every day as you move through this ongoing growth phase. The overall guiding principle introduced in Part One should be evolving into a master pearl for you. I will have repeated this pearl often enough that by the time you reach the end of the book your subconscious mind, your "little robot" as Denis Waitley refers to it, will have it stored. Once there, it will change forever the way you deal with people. The pearl is:

> "If you help enough other people get what they want,
> you'll get what you want."
> – ZIG ZIGLAR

If you have started a business or you are a principal in a start-up company and you are focused only on what you can get out of the endeavor for yourself, your leadership team and all your employees will know it's all about *you*. The prerequisite for stabilizing and anchoring your business is stabilizing and anchoring your leadership team first. It's important that sufficient time is spent making sure leaders, as they come on board, understand and buy in to the company's vision and mission, and that they have a clear understanding of the current year's revenue, headcount, and profit objectives.

There should be a broad understanding among the leadership team that focusing only on one's self and appearing to be using others to get what you want leads to failure in today's climate. Today's workforce will not work in an un-empowered environment. However, if your staff is anchored and senses you understand and believe that, "It's not about me, it's about you," then they will buy in to the business goals and objectives as well as your vision for the business, the culture, its ultimate outcome, and they will actively support you as you stabilize and anchor the company.

Time Leveraging
and Delegating

Y ou are face-to-face now with the need to think strategically. Your original business idea has proven to be sound and the business is now moving forward successfully. You should now be realizing that your original business idea was fine, but the key to growing it is not your original business idea, it's the people you surround yourself with and their motivation and focus. You must come to grips with and understand a principle that has been historically the essence of all successful enterprises—time leveraging. The pearl is:

> "Time is the most precious element of human existence.
> The successful person knows how to put energy into
> time and how to draw success from time."
> – DENIS WAITLEY

So, what do I mean by time leveraging? As an individual, you have only so much time per day to work and earn income. As you bring people into your business and your workforce expands, you have a number of people every hour working and bringing income into your business simultaneously. During the later days at CST we had 1,000 people working every day—the time leveraging result was $100 million annual revenue.

118

I'm amazed, looking back on my own career, that I did not understand this principle earlier. I worked hard and became, in my own mind, anyway, self-sufficient and very good at what I did. While it is important to hone your own skills and continue to perform personally as you grow in position and responsibility, it can become a trap as an entrepreneur. The trap comes if you are continually working on the company's contract deliverables and not spending enough time leading and motivating others to accomplish the contracts' requirements. You also may fall into the trap of telling your people how to do everything and micromanaging them instead of delegating and empowering your staff, if you are too embedded in the work.

The following example illustrates this point. When I was branch manager for a government support services company, we were developing desktop project management productivity software for a Department of Defense Weapons System Project Office. I had a lead person directing a small group that was developing the software applications. I had put in place an open-door policy, so I was close to all the team members as we made progress. At one point, as we neared the end of the project, I learned through a conversation with one of the subordinates that the lead software engineer was reviewing the programs as they came to him, taking them home at night, rewriting them, and then bringing them back and integrating them into the system.

This manager was attempting to support the project and was spending considerable personal time on it, but the problem was that he was not keeping in mind his responsibility to lead his staff, nor was he thinking beyond the current contract and encouraging his employees to develop and grow in their work performance. He was not only not growing his staff in their technical performance ability, he was discouraging them by doing their work. I sat down with him and explained how I viewed what he was doing and how his actions were being viewed by his team members. I helped him image what he was doing and why the team was reacting the way they were. He basically had an aha moment, then met with his team.

During that meeting they reached an agreement about moving forward collaboratively, which led to them completing the contract successfully.

The trap I referred to earlier boils down to having a tendency to tell people how to do something—or just doing it yourself—rather than explaining what outcome you want and letting your staff creatively achieve the result. More times than not they will achieve the outcome more effectively than you. Remember that leading is delegating, not managing.

There are numerous lessons here: learn to delegate, give the creative team members a chance to shine, do not be a bottleneck, and gain an understanding of time leveraging. The difficulty with this subject is that these obstructive habits are displayed by people with a sincere intent to help and get the job done, but the long-term effect is constraining the growth of the team members and the company. So, delegate, empower, and flourish—lead, don't manage.

Revisit Your "I Wants"

Now is the time to perform a check-up on your list of the company "I Wants" discussed in Part Two and to start holding some dream-building sessions with your leadership team and remembering what this initial company "I Wants" list included. As the company founder and leader, you alone reflect on what your original thoughts were and what you hoped would be the results of accomplishing the initial company "I Wants."

As you are reaching the stabilized and anchored phase of your company's growth, revisiting the company "I Wants" will be important because doing so will continually bring to mind where you've been and helps you to stay focused on the ultimate company objective, so revising your "I Wants" also reminds you of where you're going. As before, you now can affect the business outcomes by continually reviewing and updating these "I Wants." Take a moment to revisit *why* you launched this business and what your dream *for it* was.

The equally important objective, given the company's growth, is to assure that the expanding leadership team and its members understand the importance of the company's "I Wants." You achieve this by dedicating one staff meeting per month to revisiting the company's ultimate objective and sharing what you and your leadership team plan to gain from the liquidity event. This leads to collective buy-in to achieving the company's outcome objective. Done well, this meeting becomes a dream-building session. The important pearl is:

"People respond well to those
that are sure of what they want."
– ANNA WINTOUR

As a reminder, here is the example "I Wants" list from Part Two:

- I want the company to be profitable from the beginning.
- I want to make sure the early employees and leadership team members have well-defined personal dreams.
- I want well-formed marketing flyers ready to support early business development.
- I want to create an early company culture and establish a positive work environment that results in a great place to work.

Your company "I Wants" list will change as you continue to stabilize and anchor the company, so revisiting, redeveloping, and updating it is important as the company moves forward. Having a succinct current list of company "I Wants" supports achieving the company's ultimate liquidity objective. Examples of some ongoing or evolving company "I Wants" include:

- I want to assure the company continues to be profitable.
- I want to have moved some Task Leads to PM positions and PMs to leadership team positions.
- I want to have a well-developed and effective opportunity pipeline system.
- I want to assure that the company's culture continues to be positive and is being protected by leadership team development and growth.

Revisit Business Development and Marketing Strategy

N ow that you have your "I Wants" and dreams revisited and in order, you need to focus on revisiting your marketing strategy and new business development approach. There are a lot of great materials, CDs, and workshops on selling and marketing and I recommend you take advantage of them. My objective here will be to overlay the human element and outcome management strategies over the operational activity and drop some pearls into the dialog.

You are now at a point where you need to revisit your marketing strategy and approach. First, you need to think of strategy as a stepwise activity and not just as relating to the overall strategy of the company's reaching its ultimate vision and liquidity objective. It's a day-to-day consideration and even a moment-by-moment activity. You are making stepwise strategic decisions that move you and the company forward successfully. So, it's answering the ongoing questions:

- Where are we now?
- Do we know how to perform the next step?
- Are we clear on what the next step should be?
- How do we take the next strategic step?

Here is where you apply the SMART strategy we introduced earlier, day-by-day. If you recall, the SMART guidance includes Strategy, Motivate, Articulation, Resilience, and Transformation. So, all the SMART elements support business development and marketing. Strategic thinking leads to pursuing opportunities that fit the strategy. A motivated leadership team leads to focusing on high-win-probability opportunities. Articulating concisely your understanding of the potential client's needs leads to successful RFP responses. Resilient companies adapt their solutions to respond successfully to customers' real needs. Transformational thinking, like resilience, leads to consciously incorporating disruptive technological products and services that potential clients are seeking.

In our CST activity, Bobby and I frequently had strategic discussions to determine what would be our next logical steps. Your day-to-day and long-term marketing strategy must be developed well before launching your sales activity. The marketing concept and your short-term strategy should work to satisfy the current potential customers' needs through your products or services.

This begins by looking at the marketing discussion in your business plan and reassessing what marketing activity and material your sales team will need to optimize the plan's sales objectives. That assessment should include reviewing your market environment, your target market analysis, your website's marketing discussion and, again, what marketing material your sales activity will need. Examples of needed marketing material include:

1. A two-page Capability Statement including:
   a. Core Competencies
   b. Services and Solutions
   c. Differentiators
   d. Contract Vehicles
   e. Certifications
   f. Management Team
   g. Past Performance and Experience

2. A single-page Quad Chart that captures the Capability Statement's highlights:
   a. Upper left – Company Overview
   b. Lower left – Past Performance
   c. Upper right – Capabilities
   d. Lower right – Certifications and Contract Vehicles

3. A Capability Briefing that expands on the Capability Statement's content:
   a. Vision
   b. Chronology
   c. Key Personnel
   d. Organization
   e. Quad Chart
   f. Services
   g. Core Capabilities
   h. Contract Vehicles

4. An up-to-date website that reflects and is compatible with the Capability Statement's and Capability Briefing's content.

Relative to your sales approach, you need to refer back to your original business plan's sales and marketing strategy, assess its current validity, review the marketing material discussion, then launch your sales campaign. At this point you look for what has been defined as low-hanging fruit. That would be your business associates, your past customers, and anybody else close to you who may want to help you. After you deplete this group you will need to focus on a formal sales plan. This, on the surface, seems straightforward but it isn't. You must approach the marketing and sales strategy based on available resources. There are many approaches to moving forward so my objective here is to help you through situations you will face regardless of your approach and the current state of your company. As we mentioned earlier, the sales plan should include:

1. Executive summary and scope of the sales plan
2. Business goals and target review
3. Review of prior period performance
4. Market and industry conditions
5. Strategies, methodologies, and tactics
6. Customer segments: referrals, renewals, and new prospects
7. Team capabilities and upgrades
8. Action plans for teams and individuals
9. Performances benchmarks and monitoring

When the sales activity launches and you have identified potential opportunities, the next step is to research the opportunity's key decision makers. Then you schedule a visit to each of them and focus during these meetings on getting inside their heads and looking back at yourself and your company through their eyes. This is an application of dynamic imaging first introduced by Norman Vincent Peale in his book *Dynamic Imaging,* which is a complete study on the practice. You want to picture your potential client listening to you and looking for your solution to a problem or challenge they are having. This is one of the applicable pearls:

> "I'm not who I think I am, I'm not who you think I am,
> I'm who I think you think I am."
> – DEXTER YAGER

This strategy is sales 101 for people who understand it, but a lot of people miss this. Here is why. Your business is underway, you are excited about your product and service, and you are out selling it, but there can be a trap. The trap is that you are so excited about it that the tendency is to push your pre-established solution on anybody who will listen, including the potential customers. You are focused on your original business idea and going at the potential customer with determination explaining how great your idea is. But if you do this, you will have missed a critical opportunity to calmly ask questions, to learn how your product or service can legitimately help them, keeping in mind, as the pearl suggests, how they are viewing you.

Here is a true story to illustrate the point. At a national real estate convention a few years ago, the president of the organization was announcing annual awards. He was in the process of presenting an important award to an individual and mentioned that he had sold over three million dollars in real estate the previous year. A couple of realtors in the audience, who were not paying close attention, remarked to each other, "Well, three million isn't such a big deal. I did that much in five months last year."

After the award recipient was introduced, he stepped to the stage, accepted the award, then turned to the podium and said, "I want to thank you for this important award. It means a great deal to me since this is my first year in the business. I also must confess that I do have an advantage over most of you. You see, I'm blind and I had to learn to sell this real estate through the eyes of the buyers." The crowd was hushed for a moment then erupted into a standing ovation.

Here is another example of something to be aware of and to avoid as you are focused on selling. At this point in your evolving business, a significant deviation from your business plan and sales strategy could be disastrous. Do not be distracted by a blue bird opportunity that flies in the window. I first heard this term from a professor and director of the Small Business Development Office at the University of Alabama in Huntsville. This is truly a business-killing mistake made by many start-ups. The hypothetical situation I outline below illustrates what this is.

You have developed an intended sales plan for moving the company forward and you have been following your business plan. You are making calls, developing marketing material, and building a state-of-the-art website. You are responding to RFP responses and closing deals according to plan. Then, somebody calls with a teaming offer on a very large opportunity that is not in your focus area and projections. They tell you that, if the opportunity is won, it would satisfy your next two years' revenue objectives. This is a blue bird opportunity.

It's hard to turn your back on something that looks inviting and potentially lucrative. But here's the problem: not only do you not have time to devote to the proposal, you may ultimately realize you cannot afford to pursue it financially. And I'm not referring to the proposal cost. I'm referring here to the question that will come from the teaming partner's proposal manager and their CFO, which is, "Do you have the resources to bring on the staff and buy the material needed when we win this contract?"

If you were to get to that point you would likely go into a tailspin trying to develop a banking relationship to provide a line of credit deep enough to handle it, and you would likely need to find someone to guarantee the loan as well. You are now off your initial plan and you and your time-constrained team members are engulfed. This scenario unfolding after the company has reached significant growth may be a good thing but done too early could be a very expensive lesson learned. So, beware of the blue birds and always assess your offering focus and where your business currently is. If an opportunity does, in fact, enhance your business direction, consider it, just be prepared to realistically evaluate the impact, win or lose.

Qualified Targets

This brings us to the subject of qualified targets. At this stage you cannot afford to chase every lead and spend time on non-productive sales. The pearl here is:

> "Don't confuse activity with accomplishment."
> – DENIS WAITLEY

Earlier, I discussed the bid-no-bid process in evaluating an opportunity. As you launch your sales activity you will ultimately identify a target that you will need to apply your bid-no-bid assessment approach strategy to. Again, your bid-no-bid process is very important and will need to have been thought through and clearly defined and applied as new targets are identified. The activity associated with your approach to bid-no-bid decisions will evolve over time. I am revisiting this subject again because of its impact on successfully executing your business development and marketing strategy as discussed earlier in Part Three. In the early going, your bid-no-bid efforts may just be performed by you and one other person studying the client, the performance work statement (PWS), and the potential opportunity's deliverable requirements. As you grow you would involve your proposal manager, your HR director, your accounting manager, and the proposed project manager. The consideration would include:

1. Is there enough time to respond based on the due date?
2. Does the client know us?
3. Can we handle the requirement financially?
4. Do we have the relative experience to execute the PWS?
5. Will we need a subcontractor?
6. Should we approach a potential partner to prime it?

If it is a no-bid decision, then it's done, except you may need to save the opportunity files for later reference. If it's a bid decision, then you will enter into your proposal factory activity discussed in Part Three.

An Anecdote

A CST anecdote here is to share with you some advice on at least one consideration to think through thoroughly as you strategize on sales and marketing and growth. As we were assessing where to place some growth focus, we determined that it would be important to look at our Micro-systems Division. As a result, we finally decided to deviate from our earlier strategy of promoting from within and went outside and identified a senior individual to come on board and lead the growth of this division. This anecdote has to do with being diligent and thorough in deciding to bring a sales and marketing leader on board over an existing employee team.

We thought we had evaluated this individual thoroughly, but we missed that his basic management approach and interpersonal skills were in complete opposition to our cultural approach. In a short time, there was such strong employee feedback regarding the mismatch of his leadership and management approach that we had to let him go at great expense. The overall guidance is that as you evaluate stabilizing and anchoring your company relative to sales and marketing be diligent in the assessments and evaluations.

Product and Service Check

The objective of this section is to have you slow down and reevaluate your competition and revisit your business plan's product and service offerings sections to make sure they are still viable in the market. This is an extremely important review at this point in your company's ongoing growth as it supports stabilizing and anchoring your company.

Time has a way of obsolescing everything including your business plan and your original idea. It may be time to take advantage of using the internet to go online and look for similar product or service companies and, if you find some, do not panic. You just adjust your sales approach and collateral material and bring them up to date and distinguish yourself if possible. Keep in mind that the free enterprise system continues to be at work and that competition is good. If there's not any competition, your business idea may be a bad one. Again, the guidance here is to continually evaluate the validity of your original product and service offerings. Once you've determined that your marketing activity is sound and what you are selling is viable then you may be prepared to brand your company's profile including your products and services.

During our CST days it was hard to distinguish ourselves since we were in the IT services business along with both major and minor competitors. As part of our stabilizing and anchoring activity relative to sales and marketing, we had to assess how we had evolved and how, at that point, we were viewed from the outside by partners and potential customers. So, we went through a significant branding process and evolved our marketing approach and our image. As a result, we rolled out a new byline: "Our Mission is YOU." We did not change what we did, we just reemphasized how we did it. We were doing similar work as our competitors, so we emphasized our responsiveness and did not sell prepackaged solutions. As a pure services company rather than a product company, we asked our customers what their organization's mission and goals were, then we adapted our offerings and CST solution approaches that helped our customers accomplish *their* missions. The point is, in revisiting your product and service activity you may discover that you need to adjust your offerings or your approach to selling so that you distinguish yourself as customer focused, and then you can aggressively move into your target market sector. The applicable pearl is:

> "It's not about your fixed solutions, it's about
> supporting your customer's mission."
> – Jay Newkirk

The same review and sanity check are necessary for both services and product companies. In the case of products, investigate the competition and if there are new ones, analyze them and prepare to make product design changes, if possible, that will set you apart. The same needs to be done for your services offerings. So, the basic question is, are your product designs and services solutions still viable in the market? If so, can you protect them and produce marketing and selling approaches to be successfully competitive in your target markets?

Financial Check-up

At this stage it is important to reevaluate the financial health of the company. Your CFO and finance and accounting staff along with your CPA need to be involved. This step is one of the most difficult for some entrepreneurs who are more visionary than detail oriented. Sometimes people who are visionary almost do not want to know the financial situation. I can personally relate to this because there were times when our finance and accounting and CPA teams had to drag me kicking and scratching to the financial status meetings. Here is a very important pearl, with my modification in parenthesis:

> "Surround yourself with people better than you
> (in areas you need strengthening)."
> – RUSSELL SIMMONS

The original quote on this subject is: "Surround yourself with people better than you." That is the rule but some people reject it because they have a control mentality or have not grown personally enough to understand that you do not need to know more than the people you hire, you just need to be responsible for creating an environment in which they will flourish. Make sure that you have people around you that you have empowered to focus on the financial health of the company while you are charging toward increasing cash flow and profitability.

Another important check-up that goes hand-in-hand with financial soundness is your banking relationship(s). These relationships vary widely depending on your business type. Product vs. service businesses may need either banks with specific focus, or at least a bank with focused departments in both areas. The line-of-credit requirement for a product company is normally larger and driven mainly by raw material or component purchasing that precedes manufacturing, packaging, and shipping. Service companies are delivering hours, so their line-of-credit recovery is shorter.

An additional banking check-up issue is developing banking relationships that foster open and frequent discussions on the strategic direction you are taking your business. These banking discussions and this kind of relationship will pave the way for their response to your evolving needs as you grow. Keep in mind that your banker, like your lawyer, while supportive, will be looking at what might go wrong so you must protect your vision as they point out risks along the way. It's important to listen and take their advice and remember you are paying them to look critically at what you're doing. Do not be discouraged by their conservatism, remember that it's your company and your dream. If they point out a problem or question your intent or direction, recognize it as a challenge and an opportunity to find a solution. Here is the pearl you've seen before:

> "Don't react to what people say, react to why they said it."
> – JAY NEWKIRK

As you continue the financial check-up, include revisiting your annual forecasts and pro-formas on revenue, expenses, and cash flow. Again, this is a joint activity among you, your CPA, and your CFO and finance and accounting staff. Here, you are looking at your month-to-month performance against budget projections, and the year-to-date results which brings you face-to-face with the reality of the current financial situation.

Analyzing this information results in your continuing what you have been focusing on and possibly making important changes.

It's worth taking a short break here and really thinking about this particular set of financial check-up activities and their impact. Faced with this information you may be at one of those critical decision points in the life of your company. If the performance-to-date is not on projection, you will likely have to make some important adjustments. If the numbers are bad enough you might even be getting advice to quit or give it up. Here is one of those moments of realization and understanding where the phrase, "It's lonely at the top" comes from. You must decide. Here are two pearls back-to-back that apply:

> "Success in life comes not from holding a good hand,
> but in playing a poor hand well."
> – ROBERT LOUIS STEVENSON

> "There are two primary choices in life: to accept condi-
> tions as they exist, or accept the responsibility for changing
> them."
> – DENIS WAITLEY

You need to keep in mind that in your approach to stabilizing and anchoring your business and in reviewing your product and service offerings, you may be faced with the critical decision of continuing or not. Only you can make the decision about how to move ahead. There will be plenty of advice all around you, so it comes down to listening and processing it. These are the moments you will remember when you ultimately tell your story. Making these decisions well will test and substantiate that you are solidly positioned on the 20 percent side relative to the "20/80 rule" mentioned earlier.

Infrastructure Check-up

Infrastructure refers to your in-house computer hardware and software, production equipment, and the administrative resources your team needs to reach the goals and objectives you have defined for the organization. This is another trap for many start-up companies. There is always a funding squeeze and it seems that infrastructure is placed last on the list of things needed. Big mistake! Why? It always goes back to your people. If you have bought into the motto, "It's not about me, it's about you," your credibility with your team will be in question if you are not giving them what they need to perform and be successful. Here's a pearl:

> "When you don't invest in infrastructure,
> you are going to pay sooner or later."
> – MIKE PARKER

One of the keys to the early success in our CST operation was a decision to put infrastructure growth in place well before the need. We set a goal to grow the business to a $100M annual revenue base in ten years from the launch date. We grew the infrastructure stepwise slightly ahead of the need, which fueled the growth and motivated the team. It's important to keep in mind that your CPA and CFO will help define how much to spend and how early. They will be conservative, but the key is a balance that works for everyone.

Very important elements of the infrastructure check-up worth mentioning are the administrative processes. A critical element in achieving a stable and anchored company is to determine if the infrastructure expenditures are balanced with the investment needed to operationally propel the company forward successfully. How this is done varies significantly based on the company's product vs. services structure. It normally would be handled by a series of open discussion meetings with the various contract PMs, the CFO, the Sales and Marketing Director, and the COO. The reason these discussions need to be open is because a PM's position will be to invest in infrastructure so they can easily provide their customers' contract deliverables more effectively, while the CFO and accounting staff will be focused on minimizing infrastructure costs in favor of optimizing profitability. And in the middle of these groups, the COO will be helping the group reach a compromised and collaborative decision.

Some items to check on include: the accounting software, human resources systems, customer support systems, production control, deliverable tracking, warehouse management, and project management reporting systems.

Here's a final word on dealing with important stabilizing and anchoring decisions—it really isn't lonely at the top. As you contemplate challenges along the way it's important to spend quiet time away from any of the day-to-day operational distractions and meditate. Your dream will come back, and you will be open to new ideas and pathways to the future. This process has been characterized as arriving at a grounded state and is often referred to as being spiritually grounded, which I believe is the essence of the truth of it. I am convinced that if you go to that place, it will not be lonely at the top and will lead to the answers you will seek as you move forward in your business.

Revisit Why You're Building This Business: Your Personal "I Wants"

A s we are revisiting critical company stabilizing and anchoring processes and have discussed rethinking the company's "I Wants," it's time to perform a check-up on why you're building this business, which may actually include your personal "I Wants." It is important for you to continually revisit why you launched this business and what you had envisioned you would achieve personally by doing so. These whys and personal "I Wants" are revisited all along the way to remind you of what you and your leadership team hoped to gain personally at the liquidity event.

Included in this ongoing revisit activity is to assess how your personal whys and "I Wants" should change and grow over time. The equally important objective, given the company's growth, is to assure that the expanding leadership team and its members understand the importance of revisiting their whys.

When we were at this growth point at CST, we knew how important it was to continually revisit our whys. We knew then that when we had reached this intense growth situation we and the entire leadership team would have to focus on the tactical operational activity and the day-to-day challenges, so it was hard to be thinking about dreams, applying the human element, and even the outcome management strategy. The message here is this: we actually did continually apply these strategies and continued to hold the once-a-month motivational meetings revisiting why we were building the business and what we wanted for the company and for ourselves.

My recollection is that other companies during that time weren't doing this, and the intensity at those other companies was causing their leadership team members to become vulnerable and to start looking for somewhere else to go. So, a lot of those companies didn't make it because they were focused on the challenges, pressing their leadership teams to do more and work overtime, and they hadn't locked them down with where the company was going and what the leadership members were going to achieve personally by supporting accomplishing the company's ultimate objective. So what happened to some of those companies was that their leaders were leaving and they suddenly couldn't deliver, leading, in some cases, to company failures.

In my current work as the VP for Corporate Strategy for a small Service-Disabled Veteran Owned Small Business, I'm observing the same intensity and the all-consuming operational challenges. So, my observation during the CST days as well as today is that it is critical to continually apply these strategies. I can recall as we were applying them continually back then that doing so separated us from other companies focused on their growth.

You achieve revisiting your whys and personal "I Wants" and those of your leadership teams by dedicating one staff meeting per month to revisiting the company's ultimate objective and sharing what you plan to gain from the liquidity event. You revisit your own personal whys and "I Wants" and then open the discussion so your leadership team can share theirs. A subtle side benefit of holding these meetings and the associated discussions was that it created a break from the intense operational stress and was a welcome break. Doing this leads to collective buy-in to achieving the company's outcome objective and this meeting will have become a dream-building session. Here's the important pearl:

"Whatever you vividly imagine, ardently desire,
sincerely believe, and enthusiastically act upon . . .
must inevitably come to pass."
– PAUL J. MEYER

In closing this discussion, I want to reinforce how dream building and revisiting your whys and personal "I Wants" directly support anchoring and stabilizing the company. It refreshes our need to keep in mind that our employees are the company's most valuable assets so stabilizing and anchoring them first, especially the leadership team, is key to accomplishing stabilizing and anchoring you company. You really do have to genuinely care about helping every member of your leadership team achieve their whys and "I Wants" so at the liquidity event they will, in fact, achieve their personal objectives and realize their envisioned dreams.

PART FIVE

Accelerating Growth and Company Value

B ased on your business having reached a stabilized and anchored state, it's time to move on and accelerate toward growth. Moving on will require you to take some time and assess where you are and the current state of your company from the perspective of your original business idea and the business plan projections. Think about the following as you accelerate toward growth:

> "Success is not final, failure is not fatal:
> it is the courage to continue that counts."
> – WINSTON CHURCHILL

I think it will be important to open this section with some relevant anecdotes about our CST experience when we had reached this point in our company's approach to accelerating growth. I discussed briefly earlier how we transitioned from a Systems Engineering and Technical Assistance (SETA) type contractor to one focusing on the emerging IT market sector. It was after a colleague of mine and his associates arrived at CST. We were able to pivot because we saw a growth opportunity in the IT market that we knew was going to grow, we were agile enough to step into this emerging and evolving market sector, and we could adapt what we knew to provide solutions for what our potential customers were going to need in this market.

When we had accomplished stabilizing and anchoring CST, we stepped back and assessed what we needed to do to accelerate our growth so we could reach our corporate revenue objective within the ten-year time frame we had envisioned. That assessment initiated with making sure we had established ourselves solidly in the new information technology offering space—in our case, in the government support services market. We evaluated our current ongoing contracts, our specific IT solution offerings, our leadership team's and staff's experience in the market space, and we made sure we had the financial strength to handle an accelerated growth strategy. After concluding that we had the elements needed to do just that, we identified what we needed to do to accelerate our growth and relaunched the company.

Re-looking at our CST experience and the sequence of events that took place, our decision to move forward with an accelerated strategy was to some degree a disruptive moment in terms of IT. The term *disruptive* here means that when we came to this redirection realization we needed to reevaluate our strategic direction which was serious and we knew it would impact our focus and our operation including the new business development priorities.

When I look back on what happened to us during our company's transformation from a SETA contractor to providing information technology solutions, it brings to mind how this anecdote substantiates the importance of how the human element practice can impact ongoing positive outcomes. What happened was that my colleague remembered me and called me up when he and his team were looking for where they might go to accomplish their objectives. Because of our earlier relationship during the ATI days, my colleague had a good feeling about me and remembered that even then I was concerned about his future and what he wanted to accomplish in his career so he called *us*. My point is, the human element strategy draws people to you and it does work!

So, as you assess moving forward and accelerating your growth you need to ask yourself, Where's the industry I'm in going? and What can I do that will set me apart? While you are assessing moving forward and accelerating your growth, keep this important pearl in mind:

> "Keep one eye one the current situation
> and one eye on the future."
> – LARRY WOMACK

Networking and Optimizing Your Sphere of Influence

A s part of this accelerated growth strategy it is important to be continually networking in order to optimize taking advantage of your sphere of influence. You more than likely have an intuitive idea about the importance of networking and are attending events with networking in mind. But my guidance is that you engage in these events with an outcome objective. You aren't just wandering around and having random conversations, you are there with an intent, you are looking for the people you want a relationship with, you have your business cards ready, and your company's elevator speech is right on the edge of your tongue. Also remember that it may not be the person you are engaging with at the moment who you can help, it may be about who that person knows. Perhaps they have somebody working for them who's a PM that you could support. In other words, who do they know who you could get your solution to?

Here are two pearls to keep in mind:

> "Networking is an investment in your business.
> It takes time and when done correctly can
> yield great results for years to come."
> – DIANE HELBIG

"Your network is your net worth."
– PORTER GALE

Here is an example of how we best accomplished this in the 2020 COVID-19 pandemic environment when everyone was working from home including customers, partners, and associates. Networking in this environment required a whole new approach. We needed to attend every virtual meeting and event keeping in mind that during and after these events we would have needed to identify attendees that we would like to network with so we would follow-up with them with emails with some comments and discussion on the outcome items from the event we both attended. In other words, at every virtual event attended we would take note of who the attendees were that we purposely wanted to network with, and afterword would chase them down with an email or a call and accomplish what we would have in a real networking event

Following attending a virtual networking event, if the folks we were following up with and networking with were potential customers or partners and we were attempting to identify actual business opportunities with them, we would have to remember that these people we are engaging with virtually may not have the answers we were looking for so we would have to ask them who they recommend we talk to in their organization to further identify details of potential opportunities.

Pursuing Work

Now that you have decided to move ahead aggressively with an accelerated growth strategy, make sure in your assessment activity that you look closely at *who* your company has become and assure that what you are going to be offering your customers, moving forward, has been clearly reassessed and redefined and that you constantly assess what both your current and potential clients need now. Remember that both you and they have been evolving, so what led to success in the past may not be what's needed now. Think about the following:

> "Businesses that grow by development and
> improvement do not die."
> – HENRY FORD

> "To improve is to change,
> to be perfect is to change often."
> – WINSTON CHURCHILL

The most critical aspect of this continual assessment activity is to search diligently for where both your partners and customers are planning to move. An example comes to mind from our CST assessment activity during the later years of the 1990s. We had to constantly and technically assess where our government missile weapons systems customers were relative to what the threat environment was at the time. The environments were constantly changing and evolving (just as they do now) as a result of the constant technological advances, so we had to understand that evolution and make sure our offerings were advancing as well.

As you accelerate your growth, you must make sure that the conversations you are having with your customers and partners are focused and that they know *you* know where both you and *they* are relative to their organizational objectives and evolving missions. You must show that you know what they are working on and what challenges they are having fulfilling their objectives, including what needs they now have. As a support contractor, you can't afford to lose them because *they* realize *you* don't understand how their objectives are evolving. You must go beyond what I've discussed earlier about getting inside their head, you must take that strategy to the next level. As a reminder, let's revisit this very important technique and what I mean by "taking it to the next level."

When engaging someone in a conversation, you purposely do more than just have a dialog. You take a moment to image how this person is viewing you and contemplate what they are thinking about you. If you think about this just for a minute you will likely recall how you've experienced this with a person you've known in the past and what they know about you. So in ongoing engagements you pause for a moment and think through what they would expect you to say and you formulate the ongoing conversation in a way that fulfills your perspective of their expectation. What happens when you do this is that the other person realizes you know who they are and that you likely really care about them and that you sincerely want to help them. So, taking this concept to the next level means that you contemplate more than just what they know about your past relationship, you contemplate what you think they know about the current business and contract environment you are focusing on with them at this time. Again, this leads to them realizing that you have a feeling for where they are currently, relative to contracts and their outcome objectives.

Leadership Team and Delegation While Accelerating Growth

As we moved ahead during our CST days, we had six emerging operating groups that were each focused on their individual customer environments. As a result, we had to think through how to optimize motivating our leadership team and their PMs to rethink their leadership and management approach to growing the company more rapidly.

During our CST experience when we were at this same growth point, we realized that these separate operating groups were emerging as mini-CSTs. To some degree, we had a franchising environment emerging. The thing that struck us then was that if we were going to experience rapid growth, we had to prepare to expand and grow our leadership team. We also realized that we had to protect our culture and that we could accomplish this by growing organically and from within. The only way to do that was to promote PMs internally to leadership team positions. The PMs had been growing over time, so it was a matter of assessing the subordinate organizations and promoting the selected PMs logically. The result was that we were duplicating ourselves and those subordinate organizations became replicas of both our practices and our culture.

One of the important factors in our moving forward was to assure that as these mini-CST organizations grew, our culture of "holding hands and running" was protected. We incentivized these separately emerging organizational leadership team members by establishing a year-end bonus structure for them such that if a given operation achieved its specific annual revenue and profitability goals, that operation received half of its designated bonus. They received the other half when *all* the operating groups achieved theirs. You can imagine how important it became for everyone to work together, which led ultimately to our achieving the overall corporate revenue and profitability objectives. Our approach substantiated the following pearl:

> "Gettin' good players is easy.
> Gettin' 'em to play together is the hard part."
> – CASEY STENGEL

We figured out how to help everyone help each other, so working together didn't end up being that hard after all. We were all committed to everyone achieving their dreams and were willing to do the work necessary to support one another in that endeavor.

Growing Deep First: Watering the Roots

As you may recall from the book's introduction, my CST partner and I built a successful multi-level direct sales organization before forming CST. During those days we talked about working width and depth. After spending a few years building the multi-level business, balancing growth in width and depth became essential to longevity and ultimate success. In the case of growing CST, we applied the same strategy and made sure we balanced our width and depth growth strategy—depth first, then width. After gaining an understanding of this principle it became intuitive, but at first it was elusive and we learned to put on blinders, so we stayed focused. The pearl is:

> "Diversify only after you soundly anchor existing
> product and service offerings with leaders
> backed by leaders, three deep."
> – DEXTER YAGER

The blinders gave us tunnel vision which was and still is an attribute. This has to do with staying focused on the business at hand. The approach was to stay close to our current customers and assess what new things we could do to support them, because they knew us. We were careful not to take our offerings to new customers too aggressively over going deep with current clients. Going to new customers too soon could have the effect of diluting your human and financial resources and could drag you under. This subject is about developing the talent of saying "no" or "not now" with grace.

I hope it has dawned on you by now that building a successful business is an art. The point of growing deep simply means do not run off now that you are somewhat successful and attempt to bring in business that diversifies you before you anchor what got you to this point. Growing deep means you expand what you are already doing for your current clients and offer them something else in your offering portfolio. They know you and trust you, so sell them something else you can do for them before moving toward new clients. Make sure you have leadership team members and PMs working with your current clients that have insight into what their clients need beyond what they are doing to support them now. In short, offer a new service to your existing clients, instead of offering existing services to new clients.

The strategy here is to keep growing deep with your current client base until their level of growth has reached a point where you have three leadership team members engaged with each of your current clients. This was a strategy we used in growing our multi-level busines. We made sure we had at least three growing legs in any directly sponsored group before we left them to go wide and sponsor or work with another group. We applied this strategy at CST and made sure we had strength in our current customers before we went off and started looking wide. When you have reached that kind of current customer strength and you have three PMs in the organization, then it's time to start developing your width growth strategy, meaning that when you have reached that point you will be ready to start selling what you are doing with the current customers to new clients.

Consideration for Going Wide Commercially

As an additional note on the subject of balancing width and depth growth that might be a slight deviation from the established strategy is that during the summer of 2020 there was the impact of the COVID-19 pandemic. As a result of this kind of disruptive environment, there might be a consideration, as a government support contractor, to go wide and diversify into your local commercial market sector earlier than you might have traditionally.

The reason this might be considered is that the virtual sales environment for expanding your government support strategy requires getting to know and introducing your company to government clients that are physically away from you and difficult to get close to, even virtually. Finding the new or existing customer decision makers to whom you want to introduce your company could be difficult.

In the case of diversifying into your local commercial market area, there is the advantage of possibly reaching people who know you or realize you are physically close and can serve them effectively. However, there is a caution here that you need to be aware of. If your existing government clients' contracting offices do audits on your accounting system you will have needed to establish a separate accounting cost center in your system for the commercial customers so the government auditors don't disallow your G&A exemptions. If that did in fact happen and the audit resulted in disallowing your G&A expenditures the impact on your wrap-rate could result in you becoming non-competitive.

The other approach to overcoming this competitive impact of having the commercial business embedded in your primary government support structure is to form a separate subsidiary company with an entirely separate accounting and cost center structure. The additional caution here is to not diversify in any way that is costly or too early, causing the negative impact on your current ongoing business success.

Government Contracting Vehicles

As a government support services contractor, there is an extremely important consideration needed as you develop an accelerated growth strategy. That is that you will need to move beyond just responding to random requests for information (RFIs) and requests for proposals (RFPs) that are being released frequently by your targeted government agencies. What I'm referring to here is that you need to be responding to and winning large-ceiling Indefinite Delivery/Indefinite Quantity (IDIQ) contract vehicles. These vehicles are normally multi-award contracts that several contractors win simultaneously. After receiving the award, many government agencies can issue Task Orders (TOs) under the vehicle and, as one of the winners, you only have to compete with the other winners of that vehicle. The other reason this is an important consideration is that the time it takes a government agency to award a contract under an IDIQ TO release is shortened considerably, which is good for them and the competing contractors. The pearl is:

"Government contracting growth success is optimized by responding to multiple award task order releases rather than always responding to separate contract solicitations."

– JAY NEWKIRK

In the case of CST's successful outcome, we did in fact win one of these contracts during our accelerated growth phase. The contract was a ten-year General Services Administration (GSA) Reginal contract with 10 winning companies with a total contract ceiling of $1B. After winning this contract we reworked our proposal response infrastructure and upgraded our proposal factory and were able to turn out a 7-day proposal responding to a TO's requirements. Our proposal had the appearance of being a 45-day turnaround response and, as a result, in the first year, we were able to win 80 percent of the TOs that were released under the vehicle. That win and our successful response strategy led to us achieving our ultimate company liquidity objective.

The equivalent current government contracting environment is the GSA Contract Schedules infrastructure. (See www.gsa.gov.) There are now a number of these IDIQ GSA Schedules available for pursuit and my guidance is to look into them, study them, and position to respond and acquire one or more of these Schedules as part of your accelerated growth strategy.

Review Funding Requirements and Who You Are

We frequently come back to the subject of funding requirements because, as a creative and entrepreneurial person, you are likely driven to charge ahead, so you need to put processes and infrastructure in place to support your accelerated growth strategy. As you plan to move forward you must look at the current state of your financial status then review your three- to five-year financial projections. If you are challenged financially, do not let that stymie you. Just go to work with your bankers or investors and resolve the problem, then move on. Remember:

> "Out of need springs desire, and out of desire springs the energy and the will to win."
> – DENIS WAITLEY

So revisiting your three- to five-year projections assures they are still accurate and valid now. As you resolve some possible funding challenges, take into account the need three to five years out.

This brings to mind an applicable CST story that has to do with a significant event that occurred which turned the company around. We had grown to a fairly successful level and had plateaued. We decided we needed some outside help to evaluate how to continue to accelerate our growth. We asked to meet with the director of the Small Business Office at the University of Alabama in Huntsville (UAH) to provide us with some insight. As a result we invited the UAH director to visit us and he walked into our conference room and practically slammed the door behind him, which got everyone's attention.

My partner and I were there along with our six leadership team members. The UAH director stepped to the head of the conference table and looked around at us for a short time, then he focused on me and said, "Jay, let's say you are returning from a business trip and you run into someone at the airport who you haven't seen in ten years. If they asked you what you're doing now and you respond by saying you are working at CST where you are a cofounder and they ask what CST is all about, what do you say?"

I paused for a few moments and proceeded to stumble around with an answer, which was not very succinct. He finally stopped me. I was a little embarrassed. Then he turned to my partner and asked her the same question, which resulted in a similar reply, so he stopped her as well. He then looked around the room and said, "I know what your problem is; you don't know who you are. We're not leaving here today until we rewrite your vision and mission statements and everyone has a clear and concise elevator speech that can succinctly answer the question, 'Who is this CST?'"

We discovered that day that we had evolved from a government Systems Engineering and Technical Assistance (SETA) contractor into an IT and Network Systems company. We had been so close to and working on the tactical operational activity that we did not realize who we had become.

Revisiting Business Processes and Stabilizing the Operation

It will be important to assess your business processes relative to an accelerated growth strategy. You will have processes in place that have worked successfully getting you to this acceleration stage. The obvious question is, will they work effectively now as you refocus on rapid growth? If not, they will need to be upgraded and stabilized to accommodate the company's growth. The amount of effort and resources allocated for updating these processes should be directly proportional to your three- to -five-year goal and your ultimate exit strategy. If your objective is to grow rapidly as we did at CST, then you will need to anticipate the growth and make sure the processes and infrastructure are in place to accommodate it.

The finance and accounting function needs to be looked at first, including accounts receivable and accounts payable, cash flow analysis, payroll, and monthly reporting. When CST began to grow with multiple contracts, each with several TOs, we needed a way to track their financial status down to the task level. Our accounting package was not sophisticated enough to accommodate that need so we contacted our accounting system vendor for help. They were in the process of designing and developing the capability we needed, but it was not going to be available for a year. Our chief financial officer (CFO) and F&A manager found a third-party software vendor who had developed that capability in an application compatible with our current accounting system which would provide our project managers and task-leads the ability to monitor in real time their projects' financial status.

We bought and implemented the software that solved the problem, which worked to our advantage in several ways. The leadership team down to the task-lead level had real-time financial status on every task, which then rolled to the contract level for visibility relieving pressure on the F&A function who before was constantly being asked by the project and task leads for this information. It also took away financial visibility excuses from the technical leadership and line managers. They were now empowered and responsible for close financial management of their work. The third-party product's capability provided what we needed. It is also important for you to understand that we bought this package early enough so when the growth came and the need was serious, the capability was in place and the leadership team was prepared to implement it.

> "Don't ever let your business get ahead of the financial side of your business. Accounting, accounting, accounting. Know your numbers."
> – TILMAN J. FERTITTA

So, as you plan to accelerate growth have in place accounting contract status systems to support the growth objectives.

Now, let's revisit human resources (HR) and that function's ability to accommodate the new growth strategy. The HR processes are frequently understaffed and/or underdeveloped. A few HR issues worth mentioning include recruiting, interviewing, reference checking, and insurance account management. These functions become critical as new contracts are coming on board rapidly and some automation systems and additional personnel may be needed.

At CST we had our recruiting and interviewing processes well developed but had to make sure our leadership team members understood that we needed to protect our positive work environment and culture. So, we spent important time sharing with the leadership team members our strategy during the interview process to make sure the candidates knew we wanted to assure the job they were applying for was right for them.

Another important HR topic is insurance account management. Since we are discussing accelerating growth this topic is particularly important as the number of employees grows. Well-designed insurance benefits packages are vital to employee retention. Again, as you focus on accelerating your growth you need to reevaluate your benefits package and have processes in place to effectively manage employee insurance status and issues.

The other company administrative topic area is contract compliance and is one of the most important areas of focus for a rapidly growing business. As contracts are being negotiated and executed there is always an objective to accommodate the clients' requirements, but it will be important to write and negotiate tight contracts. Let's focus on this with an example.

My cousin, who has a small landscaping and lawn care business, entered into a contract to design and build an outdoor barbeque, stone patio, and water garden, a very elaborate and expensive project. The client was overseeing the work day-to-day and making changes along the way with verbal commitments from the customer that the costly changes would be covered at the end. Unfortunately, not only did the customer not cover the changes and upgrades, but he later claimed that the work was inferior and decided not to pay anything at all, putting my cousin's company into near bankruptcy. The work that was done was top-notch, so it was a wake-up call for my cousin who, after that, never entered into another loosely written contract. He now fully understands contract compliance.

As you accelerate your growth it will be important to consider an outsourced contract management expert to make sure your contracts are solidly constructed until you can afford to hire a contracts person with knowledge in this area.

Revisit Organizational Structure

We have discussed organizational structure before. Since you have now decided to launch an aggressive and accelerated growth strategy, revisiting your organization's structure may be critical to achieving it. We've discussed the fact that many organizational ideas and structures have evolved over time. Now that you've grown, you need to discuss the new structure in one of your planning meetings or a weekly staff meeting designated as strategic to provide the team creative input to the possible new structure. You will need to have protected your collaborative culture when you introduce your new growth strategy because your leadership team will be critically focused on the new organizational structure to make sure they aren't negatively affected by it. You want to avoid conflicts and competition taking place as a result of the new structure. There is a side benefit to holding these accelerated-growth creative planning staff meetings, which is that you will learn more about how your leadership team has evolved. Remember this pearl:

"The secret is to gang up on the problem,
rather than each other."
– THOMAS STALLKAMP

Another important point on organizational re-structure is chartsmenship. Don't update your organizational chart casually without thinking about how it is going to impact everyone as you move forward. This is important because, as you know, org-charts show everyone where they will sit in the organization. There has been a lot of controversy on organizational structures over time—flat versus vertical (hierarchical)—so as you revisit and update it, it is important that it clearly reflects your new organizational structure concept.

This is another situation where you can exercise imaging. You need to keep in mind how your leadership team is viewing you and what they may be thinking about relative to restructuring the company's organization for accelerated growth.

Thinking this through thoroughly as you develop your moving forward strategy will pay big dividends as your company and leadership team continue to grow. You will want to gain individual buy-in on your accelerated growth plans—one-on-one, if necessary—with your leadership team members before having an open discussion about your growth strategy. This will result in a positive outcome because you will have developed a broad acceptance of your growth strategy. You will have set up the organization to operate effectively moving into the accelerated growth phase. The following pearl applies:

"An organization, no matter how well designed,
is only as good as the people who live and work in it."
– DEE HOCK

So, the restructured organization and its associated org-chart will provide you and your leadership team a clear image of how you will move the company ahead rapidly. It will be very important to hold a staff meeting segment devoted to introducing the new structure and bring up the old org-chart next to the new one and explain the new structure relative to how it is transitioning from the old one. Doing that clears up any questions the leadership team may have had, and the outcome will be that everyone knows exactly how the company is going to move forward with a collaborative leadership team.

Strategic Sales and Marketing Plans

A s you continue past the stabilizing and anchoring business phase to sustained and accelerated growth including balancing width and depth pursuits, you need to take a moment to revisit your business plan's projections and revisit your strategic sales and marketing plan.

We have discussed before the importance of understanding the difference between sales and marketing. In light of your new focus on accelerated growth, you must critically evaluate your sales-supporting marketing material to assure that it provides aggressive, forward-looking images and text that capture your new growth strategy. This includes reviewing the marketing collateral material, conference booth graphics, and making sure you have updated your website to reflect this new strategy. Your marketing upgrades and assessments should include updated market research activity. Done well, these activities will successfully support the sales team, which should be focused outwardly into the company's target market sector with emphasis on the accelerated growth. Again, the upgraded and refocused strategic sales and marketing plan should encompass clear guidance in both areas and emphasize the importance of these two functions continually collaborating.

Remember while reworking your sales and marketing plan do it through imaging your company in the future through your personal dream and the dreams of your leadership team. While you work on rethinking your growth strategy, I will always bring you back to the basic success principles that lead to success. Here's a pearl to help you:

> "No man or woman is an island. To exist just
> for yourself is meaningless.
> You can achieve the most satisfaction when
> you feel related to some greater purpose in life,
> something greater than yourself."
> – DENIS WAITLEY

Waitley is pointing back to the idea that no matter where you are on your growth pursuits you have to revisit why you're doing what you're doing and it always has to be something "greater than yourself." He's referring to the dream and the, "It's not about me, it's about you" concept.

As you focus on and revisit your sales and marketing strategy you want to make sure your leadership team members honor and support protecting the positive culture you have built that got you to where you are now. You must assure that the aggressive growth strategy preserves the existing culture. It is my belief that success comes from gaining an understanding of the principles hidden in the many positive mental attitude books we've referred to and by applying the pearls of business drawn from them. Remember:

> "The winners in life think constantly in terms of I can,
> I will, and I am. Losers, on the other hand, concentrate
> their waking thoughts on what they should have
> or would have done, or what they can't do."
> – DENIS WAITLEY

Again, revisiting your sales and marketing strategy with your accelerated growth plans results in a new collaborative leadership team capable of holding hands and running. They can and should be filled with vision and inspiration. If you just treat developing these updated plans without overlaying your vision and dream onto them, the value will be lost. Your team will not be motivated by them and outsiders will not be impressed. Every time you review and reread your updated growth strategy and sales and marketing plans you should be proud and inspired.

Adding Value

Assuming your new accelerated growth strategy worked you will ultimately be approaching your liquidity event and you will need to slow down for a moment and assess your company's value. I have observed, over time, that company valuations aren't a priority for business owners while they are concentrating on growing their companies unless there is a need to raise capital. In that case, investors or business loan decision makers will perform a company evaluation.

However, as you begin to contemplate your liquidity event it is imperative to step away from your day-to-day operational activity and assess how your company is viewed and valued from outside. This takes conscious effort because your focus will have been on growing the company, dealing with operational challenges including employee and revenue growth, and profitability. Valuation is usually not in the forefront.

So, when you do realize the need to assess the company's value, you begin by revisiting your original liquidity objective and determine if that is still valid. In addition, you will need to rethink not only the company's liquidity objective but also your personal dream and objective. So, as you consider liquidating, you are assessing if the event will provide you with your original financial outcome goal. At the same time, you should revisit your leadership teams' dreams and financial goals and assure the liquidity objective meets theirs as well. You will need to get into a due diligence mindset because when it comes to liquidity, the potential buyers will, for sure, have due diligence professionals perform a conservative assessment of the company's value.

So, what areas of the company do the assessors look at to determine company value? They will look at: the leadership team, including the chief operations officer (COO) and the new business development staff; the company's revenue and profitability; current contract base; employee turnover rate; and, if you are a federal government support contractor, they will ask to see your Contractor Performance Assessment Reporting System (CPARS) reports.

Assessors will meet with the COO who will likely be a key individual transitioning to the purchasing company. They will ask his or her evaluation of their PMs and other direct reports and will tie the PMs to the contracts they are managing.

In the case of the leadership team, the assessors will ask to see their resumes, will want to know if they have ownership, and on what contracts they are overseeing. They will ask to see their performance evaluations and, finally, they will want to know their length of service with your company. They will assess the new business development staff and their processes including their new business development projections and their pipeline entries.

In the case of revenue and profitability, assessors will spend time with the CFO and look at the accounting system and spend significant time interviewing the accounting staff. There will also be time spent with the HR director assessing their recruiting processes and the employee retention rate.

Now that you know the liquidity assessment focus areas for maximizing your company's value, you will need to perform your own equivalent internal assessments as you approach the liquidity event. An important consideration would be to engage a Mergers and Acquisitions (M&A) company to assist your internal assessment. Here is an important pearl from the president and CEO of the real estate company Movement Mortgage:

"Our objective is to couple vision and value.
Bring value to people that satisfies their vision
and accomplishes our company's vision . . ."
– CASEY CRAWFORD

In the case of our CST approach to this activity, two years before we had targeted our liquidity event, our CFO suggested we hire an M&A firm to support our internal value assessment. That turned out to be a very important move on our part. This M&A firm was very knowledgeable about the evaluation process and led us to ultimately optimizing our value.

One of the significant outcome areas was the profitability assessment. We had a Microsystems Division that was selling significant computer system hardware and peripherals to the federal government at very competitive prices. They were generating big revenue numbers but the profit margins on those sales were way under the profit levels being generated by our services revenue. Our M&A team advised us to either sell that division or modify their target market and offerings to get to a margin level equal to the other divisions.

My partner and I met with our CFO to discuss the issue. We decided that instead of us deciding what to do at our level, we would meet with the division's staff to get their collective opinion on how best to move forward. That turned out to be an important move on our part. The division employees thanked us for giving them an opportunity to participate in the decision and asked us to give them some time to assess the options and get back with us. When they did, we received an enthusiastic answer. They wanted to stay with CST and adjust their sales strategy to generate profit margins equal to or greater than the services divisions. So, they stayed and accomplished transitioning their profit margins successfully and managed to retain their revenue levels. The final positive outcome from this anecdote is that at the actual liquidity event this division and its leadership team resulted in being an important value segment to the purchasing company.

This anecdote and the previous discussion have focused, to some degree, on value propositions if you are a government support contractor. However, if you are a commercial client company the guidance is much the same. The acquiring entity will be looking at the same assessment areas just as an investment firm would if you were in the process of raising money.

Introduction of Exit Strategy

As you now approach your liquidity event and have successfully accomplished accelerated growth it's time to formulate your exit strategy. This is a subject that is sometimes never mentioned during the leadership team's aggressive growth focus. Assuming you have reached that point, developing and holding to your exit strategy is crucial to your ultimate success. Here is a pearl to think about after achieving a successful liquidity event:

> "What you get by achieving your goals is not as important as what you become by achieving them."
> – ZIG ZIGLAR

This is such an important subject it's worth getting seriously focused on it here. First, this is a touchy topic for some people because it requires clearly redefining their own dreams. The reason is that the proceeds from the exit event basically define what you will personally gain financially. When you slow down long enough to think about it, you realize it's not trivial and that defining it demands serious thought and brings you to a point of contemplating what your life's ambitions have been and what you really want to achieve. A large percentage of the population struggles with the prospect of gaining significant resources or wealth because they have been taught or believe that it's bad and even sinful to seek wealth. Assuming you have overcome that, below is an important pointer on doing it well.

When you have determined what you want financially from the liquidity event for yourself, your family, and your other shareholders, then you can set a value for your company that you need to reach. Based on your anticipated growth rate, you can then calculate when you will reach that point. If the time to reach the goal is longer than desired, you may want to reassess the revenue growth objective needed to reach the value sooner. One important parameter you will need to calculate is the revenue or profit multiplier for your business and industry sector.

The close on this subject is to address why you should even think about your exit strategy right now. Well, here's why. If you have this strategy clearly defined and believe you are going to reach the objective, that will pull you through all the obstacles that will appear along the way. In addition, it will also have the same impact on your leadership team. So do it, don't be shy, be bold, and accomplish your accelerated growth objective and company value and formulate your exit strategy. I'll end with the master of all the pearls:

"If one does not know to which port one is sailing,
no wind is favorable."
– LUCIUS SENECA

Closing Thoughts

As we bring *The Pearls of Business* Book 1 to closure, I want to share some final thoughts with you. I have a sincere feeling of gratitude for you allowing me to share my guidance with you given you have or are contemplating launching your own business.

Throughout the book's offerings I have talked about applying the human element and outcome management strategies. I also have probably *worn you out* about having a clearly defined personal dream that will come true for you if you grow your business to a successful liquidity event and reap the rewards that will fuel the dream coming true.

So, in these concluding remarks it only seems right for me to share with you *my dream*. Thinking about it and looking back honestly the dream hasn't changed from the moment my partner and I sat down at the little round conference table in my den and contemplated launching our own government professional support services company. We talked about what we could offer, who our clients might be, and what we should name it.

We discussed following the business guidance we had obtained as we had built a successful multi-level marketing business and the effort we had put into convincing all of our down-line distributors that having a clearly defined dream would be key to their ultimate success.

As we were having this conversation it dawned on us that we better have our dreams in order as we launched our company. So, I jumped on it first and asked Bobby, "What is your dream?" She leaned back and smiled at me then leaned forward and said seriously, "Jay, if we can grow this company to a significant level and I receive enough out of it to become financially free I want to *give back to my people.*"

You can guess what came next. She asked me the question. I can recall the humbling feeling I had then. At that point in my life I had worked with Dr. Werner von Braun's team on the successful Apollo Program, had supported the deployment of the US Government's BMDSCOM Sight Defense system that gave Reagan the negotiating strength to shut down the Russian's cold war nuclear threat, and I had successfully grown a government technology support services branch office in Huntsville, Alabama, for a Capital Region headquartered technology company.

Looking back over time I realized that all that work and the associated success had come from helping other people accomplish their objectives. So, my answer was, "Bobby, as you know, my definition and measure of success has always been 'How many people have you helped in your lifetime?' So, *when* we achieve a significant financial outcome from our company, I want to help as many young business owners and entrepreneurs that I can reach in the time I have left."

That is still my dream and in fact is the motivation for *The Pearls of Business* books; the associated Jay Newkirk Business Consulting, LLC; and my website, www.jaynewkirk.com/ blogs, workshops, and webinars. However, my real reward is your success. Which, by the way, is very much the byline that came to Bobby and me when we were branding Computer Systems Technology, Inc. which was: ***Our mission is You.***

As a final closing note, the second book in *The Pearls of Business* series is on its way and is focused on preparing for a successful liquidity event and driving serious value into your business as you anticipate that event. In addition, there will be some extraordinarily important guidance on how to optimally bring your dream to pass with the resources you gain from the liquidity event and, most importantly, some guidance on some things to do that will be greatly rewarding including some things not to do when your mind is blown and you find yourself financially free.

My Best Wishes Are With You!

Acknowledgments

It is with profound gratitude that I acknowledge the editorial advice and support of my wife, Linda, who not only supported this book effort but positively supported and endured my persistent serial entrepreneurial ventures.

Special thanks and gratitude go to my longtime friend and colleague Ms. Bobby Bradley for her winning attitude, her dedication to the joint endeavors we pursued over the years, and her exemplary leadership skills as president and CEO that led to our successful Computer Systems Technology, Inc. (CST) liquidity event.

Thanks also to Jim Tevepaugh for his overall guidance and editing comments that enhanced the original manuscript's clarity significantly. Thanks to Daniel Tait and Michele Platt for their editorial input and Trisha Truitt who edited the original final draft and finalized that manuscript's formatting.

Additional thanks goes to our CST leadership team whose extraordinary effort led to the successful liquidity outcome: Kevin Webber, CFO; Randy Cash, COO; Jay Sullivan, CTO; Mark Edwards, VP New Business Development; Brent Beam, Sr. Exec. MicroSystems Div., and Michelle'e Korak, VP Human Resources.

Important thanks go to Larry Womack who provided Bobby and me early CST invaluable advice and guidance, for his insights while drafting the *Pearls of Business* manuscript, and also for providing the book's foreword.

A special thanks goes to Phillip Wendling, President and CEO of Government Energy Solutions, Inc., (GES) where I served as the VP for Corporate Strategy while working the *Pearls of Business* (POB) book and project. His support and my working at GES were very important, giving me up-to-date information and insight into small business challenges long after our CST liquidity event.

Additional thanks go to Dr. Debora Barnhart, Cole Walker, and Donna Coleman, members of the Energy Huntsville Initiative's Board of Directors, where I served as Executive Director and Board Chair, for their input and support while I was simultaneously developing the POB project.

Thanks also to Vicki Morris, President at Face-To-Face Marketing, for supporting my Pearls of Business Project workshops and hosting me as a guest speaker at her R.I.S.E Events. Thanks to Miranda Bouldin, President and CEO of LogiCore, for hosting me on her syndicated TV show, *The Miranda Show.*

Thanks also to Kenny Anderson, Multicultural Affairs Officer for the City of Huntsville and host of the TV Talk Show *Impact with Kenny Anderson,* for inviting me to appear on his show allowing me to share with him and his audience my POB project and book.

Additional thanks go to Ronald G. Wallace, Ret. United Parcel Service Inc.'s Executive, and Madison CEO's facilitators; Michael and Suzanne Katschke, for allowing me to feature them in two of my Jay Newkirk Business Consulting POB website's blog interview posts.

An extraordinary debt of gratitude goes to my parents, Marshall and Alice Newkirk, who I have always admired. As a very young couple in their late teens and early twenties they decided to leave their roots in central Arkansas to move to Northern Virginia, a thousand miles away, to launch their own business. Additionally, they created a positive, loving, supportive, and Christian family home environment for my brother, Robert, my sister, Janice, and me. I can remember my mother continually telling me as I was growing up that I could achieve anything I set my mind to. An extraordinary outlook for a young mother having left her home following her husband's dream and vision and harboring that positive attitude in the midst of growing global political unrest and the threat of world war.

And finally, an important acknowledgement and debt of gratitude goes to my editor, my Pearls of Business Project Manager, and my friend, Jessica Swift. Over and above her book editorial effort, she managed my Jay Newkirk Business Consulting launch, collaborated on my website, enhanced my media presence, promoted and edited my website's blog posts, and has mentored me in building a social media following leading to the successful launch of *The Pearls of Business* book.

www.ingramcontent.com/pod-product-compliance
Lightning Source LLC
Chambersburg PA
CBHW052043090426
42739CB00010B/2026